French Review

FOR READING IMPROVEMENT

French Review

FOR READING IMPROVEMENT

FRANCIS W. NACHTMANN

UNIVERSITY OF ILLINOIS

THE MACMILLAN COMPANY

COLLIER-MACMILLAN LIMITED · LONDON

printing number
8 9 10

Library of Congress catalog card number: 66–16097

THE MACMILLAN COMPANY
COLLIER-MACMILLAN CANADA, LTD., Toronto, Ontario

PRINTED IN THE UNITED STATES OF AMERICA

Preface

THE purpose of the present book is to offer the student of French
the opportunity to improve his reading ability. A basic acquain-
tance with French grammar is assumed. Most of the material
usually presented in an elementary course is reviewed, at least in
a passing way, but stress is laid on those points which cause most
difficulty to the English-speaking reader. This method may give
some impression of distortion, by comparison with the conven-
tional review grammar, but it will meet the needs of the student
who wants to improve his comprehension quickly. The treatment
of the perennial trouble spots is greatly expanded and provided
with special drills.

Ease in reading French is hardly ever a question of acquiring
specialized vocabulary in the reader's primary field of interest.
The large number of cognates shared by French and English
make the vocabulary of most fields quite accessible, and in any
case new nouns and regular verbs can be looked up in the dictionary. The difficulties of comprehension which occur with
monotonous regularity are those involving: (1) idioms, (2) verbs,
that is, identification of tenses and irregular verb forms, and (3)
certain types of vocabulary, such as the connective words and the
false cognates. Each new generation of amateur translators
includes numerous adherents of the folk-theory that the way to
learn to read French is to plunge in and read, read, read in one's
own field. The brash nonlinguist who says "Oh, I can pick up a
French book and get the thought from a page" needs only to be
called on for a demonstration to show how inadequate that
thought is. He will usually fall naïvely into every one of the
standard pitfalls: the *depuis* construction, *venir de, ne ... jamais que*,
and so on. The numerous cognates give a false sense of assurance;
it is the mortar holding the cognates together that is critical,
and most people need some guidance. While the reader may
practice his skill in his own field, the problems he is going to have
are essentially the same for all fields, from the most literary to the

most technical. This book brings those problems sharply into focus.

Each of the lessons presents a discussion of certain French constructions followed by a list of idioms, by a group of irregular verbs to be reviewed, and by exercises. Most of the exercises provide material to be translated into English, but in some of the lessons there is a short drill requiring some direct manipulation of a French sentence. This latter is often an effective device for driving a point home and aiding the memory.

The vocabulary of the exercises, except for the main points being illustrated, is generally kept simple. It is assumed that the student is doing considerable reading in other sources at the same time he is using this book.

In the Appendix, besides all the usual tables of verbs, there are two lists of the type of vocabulary indispensable to reading in any field. One is a list of prepositions, conjunctions, and adverbs. This should be memorized. If a reader can grasp the words in a passage which mean "however," "although," "on the other hand," "consequently," and so on, he immediately grasps the whole logical organization of the paragraph. Yet these are the words hardest to remember, and most students spend frustrating hours looking up the same items hundreds of times. Memorization of this list will lighten the problem of comprehension in any field as if by magic.

The second special vocabulary list in the Appendix enumerates the principal false cognates.

Also included in the Appendix is a glossary of grammatical terms for the benefit of those whose memory of these things may have become dim.

Although this review grammar is primarily designed for organized classes, particularly of graduate students seeking to improve their reading knowledge, it attempts through detailed explanations and an abundance of examples to provide material which can be used also for independent study by anyone desiring to strengthen or revitalize his reading comprehension of French.

F. W. N.

Contents

Lesson

I. Review of the Regular Conjugations; Meanings of the Indicative Tenses; the Verbs Conjugated with *Être*   1

II. The Imperfect Tense; the Past Tenses of *Vouloir*, *Pouvoir*, *Savoir*, etc.   8

III. The Present and Imperfect Tenses with *Depuis*, etc.; the Present Participle; Idiomatic Uses of the Past Participle; the Indefinite Pronoun *On*   17

IV. Reflexive Verbs   24

V. *Devoir* and *Falloir*   32

VI. Negatives   38

VII. Causative *Faire*   46

VIII. Nouns and Adjectives   52

IX. Personal Pronouns: *y* and *en*   63

X. Demonstrative Adjectives and Pronouns; Adverbs; *Tout*   71

XI. Relative Pronouns; Interrogative Pronouns; Impersonal Verbs   80

XII. Special Uses of the Future and Conditional Tenses; Conditional Sentences   87

XIII. The Subjunctive   93

XIV. Summary of Uses of *Que* and *De*; Words Often
　　　 Confused   101

Appendix A: List of Prepositions, Conjunctions, and
　　　　　　　 Adverbs   109

　　　　　　 B: False Cognates   113

　　　　　　 C: Numerals and Measurement   115

　　　　　　 D: Glossary of Grammatical Terms   119

　　　　　　 E: Verbs   123

French–English Vocabulary   149

Index   167

LESSON I

Review of the Regular Conjugations; Meanings of the Indicative Tenses; The Verbs Conjugated with Etre

[1]
REVIEW OF THE REGULAR CONJUGATIONS

REVIEW the indicative, imperative, and subjunctive forms, all tenses, of the three regular conjugations and the auxiliaries *avoir* and *être* in APPENDIX E. These tenses and their meanings should be memorized. However much time this activity may take, the student who bypasses it will later spend many times that number of hours in the far less satisfying activity of constantly checking verb forms. Moreover, the irregular verbs which are introduced in the later chapters a few at a time imply a thorough understanding of all the material that treats of the regular conjugations in the first part of APPENDIX E.

The following paragraphs present points to be emphasized in the review.

[2]
THE MEANINGS OF THE TEN INDICATIVE TENSES[1]

Seven of the ten indicative tenses can be said to have a single meaning. However, the three most commonly used—the present, the imperfect, and the past indefinite—are each equivalent to several different forms in English and only the context shows the exact meaning. The following points should be carefully observed when dealing with the tenses in question.

---

[1] The conditional and conditional perfect actually constitute a conditional mood but they are treated here as tenses of the indicative as a matter of convenience and in conformity with a well-established convention.

A] The French PRESENT tense has no special forms. English, however, has a PROGRESSIVE PRESENT (*he is studying*) and a HABITUAL PRESENT (*he studies*). In French a single form (*il étudie*) expresses both ideas. The progressive meaning is often the only one that makes sense in a given context.

Ne la dérangez pas! Elle *étudie*.	Don't disturb her. She *is studying*.
Je *vais* tenter une nouvelle expérience.	I *am going* to attempt another experiment.
L'eau *bout* déjà.	The water *is* already *boiling*.

The interrogative and negative forms of the French present tense given here with their meanings illustrate the first conjugation, but all verbs follow the same pattern.

PRESENT (INTERROGATIVE)

est-ce que je donne?	am I giving? do I give?
donnes-tu?	are you giving? do you give?
donne-t-il?	is he giving? does he give?
(*donne-t-elle? donne-t-on?*)	
donnons-nous?	are we giving? do we give?
etc.	

PRESENT (NEGATIVE)

je ne donne pas	I am not giving, do not give.
tu ne donnes pas	you are not giving, do not give.
il ne donne pas	he is not giving, does not give.
etc.	

Note that, to express interrogation, both languages depend in general on inversion (putting the subject pronoun after the verb or after the auxiliary verb), but English employs the auxiliary "do," "does" to form the interrogative of "I give," "you give," "he gives," and so on.

In French the *est-ce que* may be used instead of inversion to show the interrogative of any form; it regularly appears with the first person singular in all tenses (several inverted forms in the first person are quite common, however: *suis-je? ai-je? puis-je?*).

The insertion of the **t** in the third person singular of the French interrogative form is found in any tense or with any verb that does not already end in a **t** or a **d** in the affirmative: for example, *étudie-t-il? donna-t-il? finira-t-il?* but *finit-il? vend-il?* (in which both **d** and **t** are pronounced [t]).

B] The principal discussion of the IMPERFECT tense is reserved for Lesson II.

C] The PAST INDEFINITE has two meanings, as indicated in these five examples:

j'ai donné	I gave, have given
nous avons fini	we finished, have finished
il a été	he was, has been
ils ont eu	they had, have had
ils sont arrivés	they arrived, have arrived

It is the first meaning, the simple past, that is the more common, and the English-speaking reader must resist the tendency to translate always by the second form.

The interrogative and negative forms of the past indefinite are as follows:

PAST INDEFINITE (INTERROGATIVE)

est-ce que j'ai donné?	did I give? have I given?
as-tu donné?	did you give? have you given?
a-t-il donné?	did he give? has he given?
etc.	

PAST INDEFINITE (NEGATIVE)

je n'ai pas donné	I did not give, have not given
tu n'as pas donné	you did not give, have not given
il n'a pas donné	he did not give, has not given etc.

Note that "did I give?" "I did not give" are the interrogative and negative forms of "I gave."

[3]
DISTINGUISHING THE FUTURE FROM THE PAST DEFINITE

In first-conjugation verbs the endings of the PAST DEFINITE are identical to those of the FUTURE in the singular. The stem, however, is different. The stem of the future is the full infinitive.

PAST DEFINITE		FUTURE	
je donnai	I gave	*je donnerai*	I will give
tu donnas	you gave	*tu donneras*	you will give
il donna	he gave	*il donnera*	he will give
il forma	it formed	*il formera*	it will form
il différa	he deferred	*il différera*	he will defer

The last example illustrates a point of frequent confusion. Other similar verbs: *considérer, espérer, procurer, durer.*

[4]
DISTINGUISHING THE IMPERFECT FROM THE CONDITIONAL

These two tenses have identical endings; therefore it is the stem that indicates which of the two is being used.

IMPERFECT		CONDITIONAL	
il *donnait*	he was giving, used to give, gave	il *donnerait*	he would give
il *espérait*	he was hoping, used to hope, hoped	il *espérerait*	he would hope
ils *couraient*	they were running, used to run, ran	ils *courraient*	they would run

The CONDITIONAL tense, like the future, is formed on the infinitive or, as in *courir*, on an irregular stem, which the future also uses; this stem always ends in **r**. Confusion is sometimes the result when the stem of the imperfect also ends in **r**, as in the second and third examples.

[5]
IDENTICAL FORMS IN THE PRESENT AND PAST DEFINITE TENSES

In English certain verbs have identical forms in the present and past tenses: for example, "they burst," "I set" could be present or past, depending on the context. In French the verbs of the second conjugation and certain irregular verbs have identical forms in the singular of the present and past definite:

PRESENT		PAST DEFINITE	
je *finis*	I finish, am finishing	je *finis*	I finished
il *dit*	he says, is saying	il *dit*	he said

Many irregular verbs, however, which have infinitives like *finir* or *dire*, do not display this characteristic. Each irregular verb must be studied separately. Compare, for example, the present and past definite forms of *écrire, partir, conduire.*

PRESENT		PAST DEFINITE	
il écrit	he writes, is writing	*il écrivit*	he wrote
il part	he leaves, is leaving	*il partit*	he left
il conduit	he drives, is driving	*il conduisit*	he drove

[6]
ENGLISH EQUIVALENTS OF THE FRENCH SUBJUNCTIVE

The four SUBJUNCTIVE tenses in French should not be thought of as having any single English equivalent. They are rendered in English by a variety of constructions, often simply by the indicative. See Lesson XIII for the uses of the subjunctive.

[7]
VERBS CONJUGATED WITH ETRE

Most French verbs depend on *avoir* to form the compound tenses, and because the English use of "to have" for the same purpose is similar, little comment is required. Unlike English, however, all French reflexive verbs and certain intransitive verbs [2] combine with *être* to form the compound tenses. The reflexive verbs are discussed in Lesson IV. The following sixteen common intransitive verbs use *être*:

aller	to go	*venir*	to come
partir	to leave	*arriver*	to arrive
sortir	to go out	*entrer*	to come in, go in, enter
monter	to go up	*descendre*	to go down
naître	to be born	*mourir*	to die

revenir	to come back, return
devenir	to become
retourner	to return, go back
rentrer	to re-enter, return (home)
rester	to remain
tomber	to fall

EXAMPLES

Il est allé au cinéma.	He went (has gone) to the movies.
Ils y étaient allés sans moi.	They had gone there without me.
Elle serait partie.	She would have left.
Etes-vous retourné au laboratoire?	Did you return to the laboratory?

[2] English has vestiges of an earlier usage which was like the French. The verb "go" can still be used with the auxiliary "to be": She is gone.

This list should be committed to memory so that there will be no confusion with *être* as it is used with other past participles to form the passive voice. For example, note the different meanings of *est* and *étaient* in the following pairs of sentences:

Il *est* allé au cinéma.	He *has* gone (went) to the movies.
Il *est* perdu.	He *is* lost.
Ils *étaient* partis.	They *had* left.
Ils *étaient* désignés.	They *were* designated.

Note also that the past participles of the verbs conjugated with *être* agree with the subjects in gender and number. This holds true as well for the passive voice (see also Lesson IV, paragraph 6, and Exercise C).

The foregoing list shows only illustrations of intransitive verbs. Five of these verbs, however, can be given a different, transitive meaning and conjugated with *avoir*.

sortir	to take out	*descendre*	to take down
rentrer	to put back in	*retourner*	to turn over, around
monter	to take up, carry up		

EXAMPLES

Il a descendu mes bagages.	He brought down my luggage.
J'avais rentré la voiture dans le garage.	I had put the car back in the garage.

[8]
SPECIAL USES OF THE PRESENT TENSE

A] The word "can" is occasionally needed to render adequately the meaning of the French present tense.

Il ne trouve pas ses gants.	He cannot find his gloves. (*Literally:* He does not find his gloves.)

B] In literary style French narrative often changes from the past definite to the present. This use of the HISTORICAL PRESENT should be translated consistently by a past tense in English. Although the use of the present to describe a past action more vividly is not unknown in English, it is rare compared with its frequency in French.

EXERCISES

A. Identify the tense of each of the following verbs and translate into English. In tenses that can have more than one meaning give all the possibilities. If an interrogative form is puzzling, rearrange it first as an affirmative.

1. Ils mangent.	21. Il considéra.
2. Mangent-ils?	22. Il considérerait.
3. J'écoute.	23. Cela dura.
4. Est-ce que j'écoute?	24. Cela durera.
5. Vous avez eu.	25. Il différa.
6. Avez-vous eu?	26. Ils différèrent.
7. Il parlait.	27. Ils différeront.
8. Il ne parlait pas.	28. Il différerait.
9. Parlait-il?	29. Elle écrit.
10. Il a fini.	30. Elle partit.
11. Il n'a pas fini.	31. Ils avaient parlé.
12. A-t-il fini?	32. Ils étaient venus.
13. N'a-t-il pas fini?	33. Ils étaient frappés.
14. Ils sont montés.	34. Nous procurions.
15. Ils ne sont pas montés.	35. Nous procurerions.
16. Ils arrivèrent.	36. Il est vendu.
17. Ils arriveront.	37. Il est descendu.
18. On vendrait.	38. Elle rencontra.
19. On vendait.	39. Ils étaient entrés.
20. Il considérera.	40. Ils étaient obligés.

B. Translate the following sentences, being careful to choose the form of the English tense that fits the context.

1. Silence, s'il vous plaît. Elle chante.
2. Elle va chanter plusieurs airs d'opéra.
3. Ne me dérangez pas! J'étudie.
4. N'allez-vous pas étudier?
5. Avez-vous vu Yvonne aujourd'hui?
6. L'avez-vous vue hier?
7. Le nationalisme se développe très rapidement chez les peuples d'Afrique.
8. Il se répand aussi chez les peuples d'Asie.
9. Il faut se taire. Jean parle.
10. Qui va prendre la parole après?
11. Cet auteur perd lentement son public.
12. Etes-vous allé à son secours quand il vous a appelé?
13. Le printemps arrive et l'herbe pousse déjà.
14. Paul ne peut pas venir. Il finit ses devoirs.
15. Que faites-vous maintenant? —Je dîne.

The Imperfect Tense; The Past Tenses of Vouloir, Pouvoir, Savoir, Etc.

[1]
MEANINGS OF THE IMPERFECT TENSE

THE imperfect tense expresses several different aspects of past action, which in English are represented by a variety of verbal terms.

A] The imperfect tense may express an *incomplete or a continuing past action*.

Quand je suis entré dans sa chambre, il *étudiait*.	When I came into his room, he *was studying*.
Il *étudiait* pendant que nous *nous amusions*.	He *was studying* while we *were having* a good time.

B] The imperfect tense may express *habitual action in the past*.

Quand il était jeune, il *passait* le mois d'août à la montagne.	When he was young, *he used to spend* (or *would spend*[1]) the month of August in the mountains.

The translation "he spent," which conveys the impression of a single occasion, would be ambiguous. The imperfect tense of a French action verb can be rendered by the simple past form of the

---

[1] The word "would" has many meanings: (1) It may, as it does here, show habitual action in the past and thus indicate the same meaning as the French imperfect. (2) It may express the conditional or past future: He *would leave* if he could. They said he *would leave*. (*Il partirait s'il pouvait. On a dit qu'il partirait.*) (3) It may be an auxiliary of the subjunctive mood: I was afraid he *would leave*. (French subjunctive: *Je craignais qu'il ne partit.*) (4) It may be the past tense of the independent verb "will." The coal *would* not burn. (French: *Le charbon ne* voulait *pas brûler.*)

English verb only if some feature of the context indicates the repeated nature of the action.

EXAMPLE

Quand il était jeune, il *passait* deux mois à la montagne *tous les étés*.	When he was young he *spent* two months in the mountains *every summer* (*used to spend, would spend*).

C] The imperfect tense may express description or characterization in the past.

Elle *était* grande et belle.	She *was* tall and beautiful.
Il *parlait* anglais couramment parce qu'il avait passé cinq ans en Angleterre.	He *spoke* English fluently because he had spent five years in England.
Une allée d'arbres *entourait* le bassin.	A tree-lined walk *surrounded* the pond.

In these sentences no specific action is described, but a continuing state of things or the ability to produce an action is implied.

[2]

DISTINGUISHING THE PROGRESSIVE ASPECT OF THE IMPERFECT

The usual meanings given in textbooks for the imperfect tense are the following:

il étudiait   he was studying, used to study, studied.

The progressive meaning (*was studying*) is the one to be emphasized in action verbs. However, for verbs that express mental action, or at least no physical activity, the simple past tense in English is usually an adequate equivalent. Compare the next two columns:

il étudiait	he was studying, used to study, studied	*il croyait*	he believed, thought
il grimpait	he was climbing, used to climb, climbed	*ils voulaient*	they wanted
		nous craignions	we feared
nous parlions	we were speaking, used to speak, spoke	*elle semblait*	she seemed

[3]

THE IMPERFECT TENSE OF ACTION VERBS

Even in action verbs the French imperfect can either ·show performance or merely describe. English, however, makes a careful distinction between these meanings.

(ACTION)	Un homme *traversait* le fleuve.	A man *was crossing* the river.
(DESCRIPTION)	Un pont *traversait* le fleuve.	A bridge *crossed* the river.
(ACTION)	Après l'avoir écouté pendant quelques minutes, je me suis rendu compte qu'il *parlait* russe.	After listening to him a few minutes I realized he *was speaking* Russian.
(DESCRIPTION)	Il *parlait* couramment russe, français et anglais.	He *spoke* Russian, French, and English fluently.

[4]

THE IMPERFECT CONTRASTED WITH OTHER PAST TENSES

The most important thing to remember is that the imperfect tense does not show a single, completed past action,[2] as do the past indefinite and past definite.

SINGLE, COMPLETED PAST ACTION:[3]

PAST INDEFINITE

Il m'a parlé en anglais.

He spoke to me in English.
He has spoken to me in English.

PAST DEFINITE

Il me parla en anglais.

He spoke to me in English.

[2] Like most generalizations, this one does not cover every example that can be found, but for students whose experience in reading French is limited, it is the only safe working principle.

[3] The action may be represented as being done more than once. For instance, "He spoke to me twice in English." The main point is that it is considered as completed, as being done a specific number of times, and as being connected with specific past occasions. Do not be misled by the literal meaning of the tense title past indefinite. The French name for the tense is *passé composé* (compound past).

CONTINUING OR HABITUAL PAST ACTION, OR
DESCRIPTION: IMPERFECT

Il me parlait en anglais.	He was speaking to me in English.
	He used to speak to me in English.
	He (habitually) spoke to me in English.

In a narrative the imperfect describes the setting, whereas the past indefinite and past definite tell "what happened." In familiar, conversational style, the past indefinite is employed; in formal written style, the past definite.

The following translation of a familiar little verse into French can serve to illustrate the contrast between the two types of past tense.

Marie avait un agnelet,	Mary had a little lamb;
dont la toison était blanche comme la neige;	Its fleece was white as snow;
et partout où allait Marie,	And everywhere that Mary went
l'agnelet y allait à coup sûr.	The lamb was sure to go.

So far this is only background material. It constitutes description and habitual action; therefore, the verbs are in the imperfect tense.

Un jour il la suivit jusqu'à l'école,	It followed her to school one day,
Ce qui était défendu.	Which was against the rule;
Cela fit rire et chahuter les enfants	It made the children laugh and play
de voir un agneau en classe.	To see a lamb at school.

(In the second stanza the specific narrative starts. *Suivit* and *fit* are in the past definite because they show "what happened one day." *Etait*, on the other hand, is in the imperfect because it again refers to a habitual state of things.)

[5]

MEANINGS OF THE PAST TENSES OF *VOULOIR*, *SAVOIR*, ETC.

Because the imperfect shows habitual action or a habitual state of things and the past definite and past indefinite show specific action, it is necessary with some verbs to use special wording in English to convey their meaning accurately: *vouloir, savoir, pouvoir, connaître,* and *valoir* are conspicuous examples.

Il voulait partir.	He wanted to leave.
Il ne voulait pas partir.	He did not want to leave.

(The imperfect shows a state of mind not necessarily expressed by any action.)

Il a voulu partir. ⎫ Il voulut partir. ⎭	⎧ He insisted on leaving. ⎨ He tried to leave. ⎩ He started to leave.
Il n'a pas voulu partir. ⎫ Il ne voulut pas partir. ⎭	He refused to leave.

(The state of mind is expressed by an action.)

Nous savions toute l'histoire.	We knew the whole story.

(The mere possession of the knowledge is stated.)

Nous avons su toute l'histoire.	We found out the whole story.

(Stress is placed on the act by which the knowledge is gained.)

Nous le connaissions à Paris.	We knew him in Paris.
Nous l'avons connu à Paris.	We met (became acquainted with) him in Paris.
Il pouvait s'évader.	He was able to escape (but did not try to).
Il put s'évader.	He succeeded in escaping ("was able to escape" is also acceptable in English for this meaning).
Son livre valait cinquante francs.	His book was worth fifty francs.
Son livre lui a valu un prix.	His book won him a prize.

[6]

COMMON ERRORS TO BE AVOIDED IN TRANSLATING THE IMPERFECT TENSE

The imperfect tense is the object of much awkward misinterpretation by the English-speaking reader. The following are errors that occur most frequently:

(1) Failure to remember that the imperfect has the progressive meaning, particularly in verbs of physical action: "was reading," "were working," "was taking a walk."

(2) Failure to remember that "would" can show habitual past action in English and sometimes *must* be used to convey the idea of the French imperfect adequately.

[7]
IRREGULAR VERBS

Review the parts of the irregular verbs *pouvoir*, *vouloir*, *savoir*, *connaître*, and *valoir* in APPENDIX E.

[8]
IDIOMS

pouvoir   to be able (can, may, could, might)

The meanings "may," "may have," "might" for the various tenses of this verb are often overlooked, but they are the only English translations that make sense in certain contexts. Note the following examples:

Puis-je vous expliquer cela?	May I explain that to you?
L'éprouvette a pu tomber.	The test tube may have fallen.

je peux, je puis. This verb has alternate forms in the first person singular of the present tense. The second form is more common in the interrogative: *Puis-je?*

pouvant. The present participle is often used when English requires a clause.

La lettre, pouvant être mal interprétée, fut détruite.	The letter, which was capable of being misinterpreted (which could have been misinterpreted) was destroyed.

il se peut: it is possible.

vouloir   to want

In the conditional and conditional perfect tenses this verb means "would like," "would have liked."

Il voudrait devenir physicien.	He would like to become a physicist.
Nous aurions voulu poursuivre nos recherches.	We would have liked to continue our research.

"Will" and "would" are sometimes the meanings of the present and imperfect tenses, respectively.

Voulez-vous signer?	Will you sign?
Le charbon ne voulait pas brûler.	The coal would not burn.

vouloir bien: to be willing, to consent.

Je voulais bien accepter ces données.	I was willing to accept those data.
Cet éminent astronome a bien voulu nous communiquer ses impressions là-dessus.	This eminent astronomer has kindly consented to communicate to us his impressions on the subject.

This idiom, as in *vouloir* and *savoir*, shows a mental action in the imperfect ("willing") and action ("consented") in the past indefinite.

vouloir dire: to mean.

Sa réponse veut dire qu'il n'en sait rien.	His answer means that he knows nothing about it.

en vouloir à: to bear a grudge against, to be angry at.

Le chien en veut au facteur.	The dog has a grudge against the mailman.
Pourquoi lui en veut-il?	Why has he a grudge against him?

savoir   to know; to know how to, to be able (can, could)

The meanings "to know how," "to be able" apply when *savoir* is followed by an infinitive. Particularly frequent is the negative conditional tense in the meaning "cannot."

Il ne sait pas lire le thermomètre.	He does not know how to read (cannot read) the thermometer.
Je ne saurais vous le dire.	I cannot tell you.

Savoir does not require the *pas* in the negative (see Lesson VI, paragraph 9).

Il ne sait que faire.	He does not know what to do.

Not to be confused with *ne ... que*, meaning "only."

à savoir: namely

connaître   to know, to be acquainted with, to become acquainted with, to experience (especially in past definite and indefinite)

se connaître en, s'y connaître en: to know all about, to be a good judge of.

s'y connaître: to know all about it (them).

Il s'y connaît en chimie syn-thétique.	He is an expert in synthetic chemistry.
Il s'y connaît en chevaux.	He is a good judge of horses.
Son fils s'y connaît aussi.	His son is a good judge of them, too

EXERCISES

A. Translate the following sentences. Note particularly the examples of the imperfect tense and its contrast with the other past tenses employed.

1. J'ai demandé à la petite fille pourquoi elle pleurait. Elle m'a répondu qu'elle pleurait parce qu'elle avait perdu son petit chien. Plus tard j'ai su que ce n'était pas vrai. Elle n'avait pas de petit chien. Elle boudait parce que sa mère l'avait grondée.
2. Le sol tremblait déjà. La locomotive venait droit sur nous.
3. Ma grand'mère vivait à la campagne, où elle élevait des poulets et cultivait des fleurs.
4. Le professeur m'a dit qu'il préparait sa conférence. Mais il ne pouvait continuer son travail parce qu'il se sentait un peu malade.
5. Ma cousine me semblait pâle. Je croyais qu'elle était malade, qu'elle allait peut-être s'évanouir.
6. Le guide m'a parlé en anglais, mais je savais qu'il parlait également français.
7. Déjà la fumée s'élevait. On allait bientôt voir le feu.
8. Cette année-ci je ne le vois plus, alors que l'année passée il venait me voir.
9. L'année passée il est venu me voir.
10. L'astronome cherchait tout autre chose quand il a fait cette découverte.
11. Quand le jeune étranger perdait au tennis, il jetait furieusement sa raquette en l'air.
12. Chaque fois que mon collègue me voyait, il me disait quelque chose en arabe, la langue qu'il étudiait à cette époque.
13. En même temps que le réseau ferroviaire s'étendait, la technique se perfectionnait sans cesse.
14. Quand l'ingénieur en chef visitait la mine, il amenait avec lui deux ou trois inspecteurs.
15. Pendant que vous causiez, nous finissions notre expérience.

B. Translate the following sentences into English. Give special attention to the expressions in italics.

1. Nous *voudrions* voir le directeur de l'Institut.
2. Ne nous parlez pas de l'enseignement américain! *Nous nous y connaissons.*
3. Nous *ne saurions* expliquer ce phénomène.

4. — Pourquoi votre collègue *vous en veut-il?*
— Mes propos *ont pu* le *froisser.* Autrement je ne sais pas pourquoi il *m'en veut.*
5. Le savant *voulait bien* nous parler de ses recherches.
6. Il *a bien voulu* nous faire visiter son laboratoire.
7. Les œuvres de sa jeunesse, *pouvant* donner une toute autre impression de sa personnalité, ne furent jamais publiées.
8. Jean *ne voulait pas dire* qu'il allait étudier la physique.
9. Les Dupont *n'ont pas voulu* nous recevoir. Maintenant *nous ne savons que faire.*
10. *Il se peut* qu'ils *veuillent* vous punir.
11. Nous *aurions voulu savoir* interpréter les données d'une façon plus satisfaisante.
12. Nos étudiants *auraient voulu* aborder des problèmes plus compliqués.
13. Les cartes de la lune, présentées dans le livre *Sélénographie* de Jean Hevelius, *lui ont valu* le titre d'initiateur de la cartographie lunaire.
14. En 1952 des aviateurs expérimentèrent le passage du mur du son au-dessus de Paris et toute la capitale *connut* le bruit violent produit par cet exploit supersonique.
15. Les trois principaux secteurs de l'industrie, *à savoir* les métaux, les minéraux industriels et les combustibles, ont enregistré des hausses intéressantes.
16. Ce rapide exposé *a voulu* montrer combien ces phénomènes sont divers.

C. Translate into French the English words enclosed in parentheses in the following sentences.

1. Mon camarade de chambre (*was talking*).
2. Deux petits bateaux (*were crossing*) la rivière.
3. Jean et Claude (*are willing*) vous céder leur place.
4. Qu'est-ce que ce mot (*means*)?
5. Je (*refused*) l'accompagner. (Use *vouloir.*)

The Present and Imperfect Tenses with Depuis, etc.; The Present Participle; Idiomatic Uses of the Past Participle; The Indefinite Pronoun On

[1]
SPECIAL USE OF THE PRESENT AND IMPERFECT TENSES WITH *DEPUIS*, ETC.

A] With *depuis, il y a ... que, voilà ... que* + an expression of time, the French present tense is rendered by the English present perfect.

J'étudie le français depuis cinq ans.	I have studied (have been studying) French for five years.
Depuis ce jour nous y pensons souvent.	Since that day we have thought about it often.
Il y a dix minutes qu'il me surveille.	He has been watching me for ten minutes.
Depuis quand travaillez-vous?	How long have you been working?
Il mange bien depuis sa guérison.	He has been eating (has eaten) well since his recovery.

These statements concern an action or state that started in the past and is continuing in the present or up to the present; in other words, two time elements are involved. French uses the present tense and relates it to the past by means of *depuis* or the equivalent phrases. The present perfect tense in English, particularly in the progressive form, shows just such an action or state.

B] With *depuis, il y avait ... que, voilà ... que* + an expression of time, the French imperfect is rendered by the English pluperfect, usually in the progressive form.

J'étudiais le français depuis cinq ans.	I had been studying French for five years.
Il y avait dix minutes qu'il me surveillait.	He had been watching me for ten minutes.
Depuis quand était-il là?	How long had he been there?

[2]
THE PRESENT PARTICIPLE

The present participle is often preceded in French by *en* or *tout en*. These expressions can be translated (1) "while," (2) "by," or (3) omitted in translation, depending on the context. Occasionally the meaning is "in" or "on." *Tout* in this expression can be ignored, except that it usually narrows the meaning to "while" (sometimes "although").

En combinant 2 g. d'hydrogène et 16 g. d'oxygène on obtient 18 g. d'eau.	By combining 2 grams of hydrogen and 16 grams of oxygen you get 18 grams of water.
En passant par la Lorraine, j'ai rencontré trois capitaines.	While passing through Lorraine, I met three captains.
Entrez, monsieur, dit-il, en ouvrant la porte.	"Come in, sir," he said, opening the door.
Ce discours, tout en étant amusant, était déplorable au point de vue psychologique.	This speech, although amusing, was deplorable from the psychological point of view.

[3]
THE INFINITIVE USED AFTER A PREPOSITION

The verb form used after any preposition except *en* is the infinitive, whereas English uses a gerund (verbal noun, ending in *ing*) in most cases.

Sans dissoudre l'azote...	Without dissolving the nitrogen...
Avant d'utiliser l'appareil...	Before using the device...
Par peur de l'offenser...	For fear of offending him...
J'ai passé le temps à lire.	I spent the time (in) reading.

[4]
IDIOMATIC USES OF THE PAST PARTICIPLE

There are cases in which French uses the past participle whereas English uses the present participle or prefers a full clause.

Arrivé à Lyon, il s'installa dans un joli appartement.	Arriving in Lyon, he moved into a pretty apartment. (Also, "having arrived" or "after he arrived.")
Partis ensemble, ils ont suivi des chemins parallèles.	Starting out together, they followed parallel courses.
Une fois descendus, ils ne pouvaient plus remonter.	Once they had got down, they could not climb up again.
Penché à la fenêtre, Robert attendait leur retour.	Leaning out the window, Robert awaited their return.

Note that the first three examples show participles of intransitive verbs conjugated with *être*. It is these verbs (see list, Lesson I, paragraph 7) whose past participles are most frequently used in this way.

[5]
THE INDEFINITE PRONOUN *ON*

The indefinite pronoun *on* is always combined with the third person singular of the verb because to the French mind the idea "one" is singular; however, *on* is the equivalent of a number of indefinite expressions in English, several of which are plural: "one," "we," "you," "they," "people," "someone." The English indefinite "one" should be employed only sparingly to translate its French cognate because of the stilted effect in modern English. The best equivalent of the *on* construction is generally a sentence in the passive voice.

Où peut-*on* toucher un chèque?	Where can *one* (we, you, a person) cash a check?
Nous voulons aller à l'opéra. *On* joue *Faust* demain soir.	We want to go to the opera. *They* are playing *Faust* tomorrow night.
Le château est ouvert. Peut-*on* y entrer?	The chateau is open. May *we* go in?
Je dois chercher une autre place. *On* a pris la mienne.	I have to find another seat. *Someone* has taken mine.
Tout ce que *l'on* imaginait de plausible était aussitôt mis à l'épreuve.	Every plausible idea that was conceived (every plausible thing that *anyone* thought up) was immediately tried out.
Que dira-t-*on*?	What will *people* say?
C'est dans cette salle que *l'on* dîne.	This is the room in which *dinner is served.*

On avait soumis ce produit au traitement thermique nécessaire pour assurer sa stérilité.	This product had been subjected to the thermal treatment necessary to ensure its sterility.

Note that *on* and *l'on* have the same meaning. *L'on* is often used if the preceding word ends in a vowel.

[6]
IRREGULAR VERBS

Review the parts of the irregular verbs *mettre, voir, écrire, aller* in APPENDIX E.

[7]
IDIOMS

il y a: ago.

Je lui ai écrit il y a trois jours.	I wrote to him three days ago.
Il y a deux siècles, la France était toujours une monarchie.	Two centuries ago France was still a monarchy.

Note that this idiom differs from the one mentioned in paragraph 1a in that (1) its position in the sentence is flexible, (2) there is usually no *que*, and (3) *il y a* is used with past tenses.

se mettre à (+inf.): to begin (= *commencer à*).

Ils se mirent à parler.	They began to speak.

(Note that without the infinitive the expression does not mean "to begin": *Il s'est mis près de la porte.* He placed himself near the door.)

Mettre and its corresponding noun *la mise* occur in a number of combinations with *en* (or *à*) followed by a noun, which are often translatable into English by a single verb or noun.

mettre en valeur	to develop, to exploit, to put into production; to emphasize (a word)
la mise en valeur	development
mettre au point	to clarify, to narrow a question to its essentials, to restate a question; to perfect (an invention)

la mise au point	clarification, restatement of the question; perfecting, progressive improvement
mettre en œuvre	to put into effect, to put into action, to implement
la mise en œuvre	putting into effect, implementation
mettre en scène	to stage
la mise en scène	staging
le metteur en scène	director
mettre en marche	to start; to run
la mise en marche	running (for example, *les jours de mise en marche des trains*); starting
mettre en liberté	to free, to release, to liberate
la mise en liberté	freeing, release, liberating
mettre en accusation	to indict
la mise en accusation	indictment
mettre en jugement	to bring to trial
la mise en jugement	trial
mettre en commun	to pool
la mise en commun	pooling
mettre au courant	to inform

EXERCISES

A. Irregular verbs. Identify the tense and translate.

1. On met.
2. On mit.
3. Il écrit.
4. Il écrivit.
5. Avez-vous mis?
6. Ils écriraient.
7. Ils mirent.
8. Ils n'écriront pas.
9. Ils n'écrivirent pas.
10. Il soumettra.
11. Nous transmîmes.
12. Bien qu'il aille...
13. Ils vont.
14. Elles iraient.
15. Elle voit.
16. Elle vit.
17. Elle verra.
18. Ils omirent.
19. Ils ne commirent pas.
20. On permit.

B. Translate.

1. Je vais à l'école.
2. Je vais à l'école depuis cinq ans.
3. Depuis combien de temps étudie-t-il?
4. Il étudie depuis deux heures et demie.
5. Le village s'accroche à la colline.
6. Il y a des siècles que le village s'accroche à la colline.
7. Le village est tombé en ruines il y a des siècles.
8. Ils regardent ce nouveau tableau.

9. Ils ont regardé ce nouveau tableau.
10. Voilà une heure et demie qu'ils regardent ce tableau.
11. J'allais à l'école.
12. J'allais à l'école depuis seize ans.
13. Elle était couturière.
14. Elle était couturière depuis huit ans.
15. Il y avait trente ans que sa mère était couturière.
16. Il y a trente ans, sa mère était une couturière très connue.
17. Il habitait une grande maison rue Lamartine.
18. Voilà vingt ans qu'il habitait cette grande maison.
19. Il s'y est installé il y a longtemps.
20. On sait depuis plusieurs centaines d'années que des météorites arrivent parfois jusqu'à la terre.

C. Translate into English, rendering the *on* construction in as many ways as the context permits. Be sure to include the passive voice whenever it is suitable.

1. Où a-t-on mis l'encre et le papier?
2. Pardon, monsieur, on vous demande.
3. Qu'est-ce qu'on dira en entendant cette histoire?
4. Je vais vous montrer de quelle manière on écrit l'arabe.
5. Les étudiants écrivirent la leçon qu'on leur avait donnée.

D. Translate. In this and all subsequent exercises as many words as possible are introduced from the lists in APPENDIX A and APPENDIX B. These lists should be studied repeatedly until they have become thoroughly familiar.

1. Revenue pour huit jours dans sa ville natale, la célèbre comédienne est allée voir tous ses amis de jeunesse.
2. L'ambassadeur refusa leur invitation, en prétextant qu'il était malade.
3. L'officier a donné sa démission de l'armée. Le gouvernement l'a acceptée, tout en affirmant sa bonne opinion de ses services.
4. En voulez-vous? me dit-il en m'offrant du vin.
5. C'est une équipe d'athlètes, venus de France pour participer aux matchs.
6. Il grandissait rapidement et son esprit, devenu plus éveillé, s'intéressait à tout.
7. Le prisonnier fut vite mis en accusation.
8. Le gouvernement compte mettre en valeur toutes ces terres moins fertiles.
9. La communauté européenne a beaucoup profité de la mise en commun de ses ressources.
10. Nous écrivions depuis une heure.
11. Il faut que nous écrivions un compte-rendu de notre expérience.
12. Il fallait qu'ils lui remissent la lettre.
13. Elle sera mise en accusation demain.
14. La mise en scène était parfaite.
15. On l'avait mise en liberté.

16. La solution d'un acide dans l'eau est électrolysable avec mise en liberté d'hydrogène à la cathode.

17. Les hydrates de soude et de chaux se combinent avec l'acide chlorhydrique en dégageant beaucoup de chaleur.

18. Recommençons l'expérience en plaçant du sel de cuisine au fond du flacon et de l'eau dans l'éprouvette.

19. En suivant les règles de la nomenclature on donne aux corps composés des noms formés en utilisant les noms des éléments qu'ils renferment.

20. Chaque fois qu'on reproduit un corps composé en partant de ses éléments, on fait une *synthèse*.

21. Après dix années de recherche et de mise au point, les astronomes de l'Observatoire ont réalisé un nouvel instrument photographique.

22. La mise sur orbite autour de la terre du premier satellite occupé par un homme a marqué la naissance de l'ère spatiale.

23. Certaines roches lunaires de formation plus récente sont surtout des matériaux fragmentés éjectés par la force des explosions des météorites et des roches volcaniques sorties d'orifices situés près de quelques-uns des principaux cratères.

24. A l'occasion de la remise en état du réseau ferroviaire, détruit à près de 50% pendant la guerre, de grands centres de triages spécialement équipés ont été aménagés.

25. Nous avons passé l'été à nous entraîner pour les sports d'automne.

Reflexive Verbs

REFLEXIVE verbs are those that describe the action as being performed on the subject of the verb or, to put it in other words, those that have the same person or thing as both subject and object. Reflexive construction is not uncommon in English. For example:

> He considers himself an expert on the subject.
> She hurt herself.
> The ship finally righted itself.

[1]
MEANINGS OF FRENCH REFLEXIVE VERBS

The reflexive verb in French is used much more frequently than in English and is rendered by a variety of English constructions.

A] Occasionally English has an equivalent reflexive construction.

Il s'est distingué dans le domaine de la littérature.	He has distinguished himself in the field of literature.

B] Sometimes the reflexive pronoun can be simply omitted in translation.

Il se baigne, se rase et s'habille.	He bathes, shaves, and dresses.
Nous nous spécialisons dans l'art moderne.	We are specializing in modern art.
Les deux éléments se sont combinés.	The two elements have combined.

C] The reflexive is a common substitute for the passive voice. (The verbs used in the examples are *dégager*, to release; *ramener*, to bring back, to reduce; *effectuer*, to carry out.)

Quand on réchauffe ce liquide, un gaz inodore s'en dégage.	When this liquid is heated, an odorless gas is released.

Toutes ses difficultés se ramènent à ceci: il est incroyablement égoïste.	All his difficulties can be reduced to this: he is incredibly selfish.
Ces changements se sont effectués très rapidement.	These changes were carried out very rapidly.

D] In many cases the French reflexive verb must be converted into English by a construction quite different from that used to translate the nonreflexive form. Study the list of common verbs which follows.

amuser	to amuse	*s'amuser*	to have a good time
appeler	to call	*s'appeler*	to be named
battre	to beat, strike	*se battre*	to fight
demander	to ask	*se demander*	to wonder
exercer	to exercise, to exert	*s'exercer*	to operate; to practice
lever	to raise	*se lever*	to get up, rise
marier	to marry; to perform a marriage (as a clergyman)	*se marier*	to get married
plaindre	to pity	*se plaindre*	to complain
porter	to carry, bear	*se porter*	to be (in health)
produire	to produce	*se produire*	to occur
promener	to take (a person or an animal) for a walk; to move (something) along or over	*se promener*	to take a walk
rendre	to give back; to render, make	*se rendre*	to go; to surrender
retourner	to return, go back	*se retourner*	to turn around
sauver	to save	*se sauver*	to run away
tromper	to deceive	*se tromper*	to make a mistake
trouver	to find	*se trouver*	to be located, to be
agir	to act	*il s'agit de* (*impers.*)	it is a question of

EXAMPLES

Je me demande pourquoi il s'est sauvé.	I wonder why he ran away.
Il se rendra à Genève.	He will go to Geneva.
Mon frère se porte bien.	My brother is well.
La Sorbonne se trouve sur la rive gauche de la Seine.	The Sorbonne is (is located) on the left bank of the Seine.
Il s'appelait Jean.	He was named John. (His name was John.)

In the preceding list of reflexive verbs particular attention should be paid to *se battre, se retourner, se sauver, se rendre, se plaindre*, which give a false meaning or nonsense if the reflexive pronoun is translated literally.

[2]
REFLEXIVE AND RECIPROCAL PRONOUNS

A] The pronoun objects used with reflexive verbs may take the following forms:

> *me*   myself
> *te*   yourself
> *se*   himself, herself, itself, oneself, themselves
> *nous* ourselves
> *vous* yourself, yourselves

Because these same forms may serve as indirect objects they may also mean "to myself," "to yourself," and so on.

B] The pronoun objects *nous*, *vous*, and *se* may also be used in the reciprocal meaning "one another," "to one another," "each other," and "to each other."

Nous nous connaissons depuis dix ans.	We have known each other for ten years.
Ils se sont écrit beaucoup de lettres.	They have written many letters to each other.
Quand on se connaît, on s'amuse davantage.	When people know one another, they have a better time.

The reciprocal meaning may be reinforced by the addition of the phrases *l'un(e) l'autre*, *l'un(e) à l'autre*, *les un(e)s les autres*, and *les un(e)s aux autres*.

Ils se flattent l'un l'autre.	They flatter each other.
Ils se parlent les uns aux autres.	They talk to one another.

[3]
USE OF THE AUXILIARY ETRE

A distinctive characteristic of the French reflexive verb is that it is conjugated with *être* in the compound tenses. Observe the following verbs, used first nonreflexively, then reflexively.

J'ai lavé la voiture.	I washed the car.
Je me suis lavé.	I washed (myself).

Il avait coupé la corde.	He had cut the string.
Il s'était coupé.	He had cut himself.
On aurait rendu le livre.	They would have returned the book.
On se serait rendu.	They would have surrendered.

The auxiliary is *être*, whether the reflexive (or reciprocal) object is direct or indirect. However, the past participle behaves differently with the two kinds of object: ~~it agrees with a direct but not with an indirect object~~

DIRECT OBJECT

| Ils se sont vu*s* dans la glace. | They saw themselves in the mirror. |
| Elle s'est coup*ée*. | She cut herself. |

INDIRECT OBJECT

| Ils se sont écrit des lettres. | They wrote letters to each other. |
| Elle s'est coupé le doigt. | She cut her finger. |

[4]
REFLEXIVE INFINITIVES

Infinitives of reflexive verbs as quoted alone appear with the pronoun *se*, but as used in a sentence the reflexive pronoun agrees in person and number with the subject.

se promener: to take a walk.

Il va *se promener*.	He is going *to take a walk*.
Vous allez *vous promener*.	You are going *to take a walk*.
Est-ce que je vais *me promener*?	Am I going *to take a walk*?

se lever: to get up.

| Nous voulions *nous lever*. | We wanted *to get up*. |
| Auriez-vous pu *vous lever*? | Could you have got up? (Would you have been able *to get up*?) |

[5]
REFLEXIVE VERBS IN THE INTERROGATIVE AND IMPERATIVE

The rules about the position of the pronoun subjects and objects are restated in the following sentences, with examples of their application to reflexive verbs.

A] In interrogative word order the pronoun subject follows the verb or the auxiliary verb and is attached to it by a hyphen (*Allez-vous à Paris? A-t-il vu le musée?*).

Vous vous souvenez de sa sœur.   You remember his sister.

Vous souvenez-vous de sa   Do you remember his sister?
sœur?

Nous nous sommes amusés.   We had a good time.

Nous sommes-nous amusés?   Did we have a good time?

B] As for the position of pronoun objects, they come before the verb except in affirmative commands, when they follow and are connected with the verb by a hyphen (*Il* le *donne à son ami. Donnez-*le *à votre ami. Ne* le *donnez pas à votre ami*).

Vous vous asseyez toujours ici!   You always sit here.

Asseyez-vous ici!   Sit down here!

Ne vous asseyez pas ici!   Do not sit here!

Nous nous reposons.   We are resting.

Reposons-nous.   Let's rest.

Ne nous reposons pas.   Let's not rest.

Observe that in commands, in French as in English, there is no expressed subject (although spoken English tends to put it back in for emphasis: *you* sit here!). The *nous* or *vous* here is an object which follows the verb in an affirmative command and precedes it in a negative command.

[6]
TRANSLATION OF THE VERB *ETRE*

The verbs that use *être* to form the compound tenses are the sixteen intransitive verbs reviewed in Lesson I and all reflexive verbs. *Etre* in these cases serves the same function as the auxiliary *avoir* and can be translated the same way. On the other hand, *être* often appears with a past participle used as an adjective or to form the passive voice and can be translated literally. It is helpful to remember this rule: *Translate the verb* être *literally except when it is used* (1) *with one of the intransitive verbs from the special list of sixteen* (*see page* 5) *or* (2) *with a reflexive verb.*

ÊTRE (translated literally)

Il est marié.	He is married.
Ils étaient battus.	They were beaten.
Elle serait sauvée.	She would be saved.

ÊTRE = AVOIR

Elle est entrée.	She entered (has entered).
Je suis revenu.	I came back (have come back).
Il s'est marié.	He got married (has got married).
Ils s'étaient battus.	They had fought.
Elle se serait sauvée.	She would have run away.

[7]
IRREGULAR VERBS

Review the irregular verbs *venir* and *tenir* and their compounds in APPENDIX E.

[8]
IDIOMS

venir de (+inf.): to have just (used only in the present and imperfect).

Il vient de s'asseoir.	He has just sat down.
Il venait de s'asseoir.	He had just sat down.

This idiom resembles the *depuis* (*il y a ... que*, *il y avait ... que*) construction presented in the preceding chapter in that it occurs in only two tenses. The present and imperfect with *depuis* show what *has* been going on or what *had* been going on, whereas with *venir de* these tenses show an action which *has* just been completed or which *had* just been completed.

tenir à: to insist on, be anxious to; to be fond of, set great store by; to be due to.

Il tient à ses livres.	He is very fond of his books.
Il y tient.	He is fond of them.

Il tint à partir.	He insisted upon setting out.
Cela tient à la complexité de la vie urbaine.	That is due to the complexity of city life.
Cela tient à ce que le problème n'a pas été résolu.	That is due to the fact that the problem has not been resolved.

s'en tenir à: to stick to, to abide by.

Je m'en suis tenu à ces principes.	I stuck to these principles.

tenir compte de: to take into account.

EXERCISES

A. Reflexive verb forms. Identify the tense and translate.

1. Il se lève.
2. Il s'est levé.
3. Il s'était levé.
4. Il se sera levé.
5. Il se serait levé.
6. Je doute qu'il se soit levé.
7. Je me marie.
8. Je me suis marié.
9. Je me serais marié.
10. On se demande.
11. On s'était demandé.
12. Ils se battent.
13. Ils se seraient battus.
14. Nous ne voulions pas nous battre.
15. Battez-vous!
16. Ne vous battez pas!
17. Vous battez-vous?
18. Vous promenez-vous?
19. Ne vous promenez-vous pas?
20. Ne vous promenez pas!
21. Vous êtes-vous plaint?
22. Ne vous êtes-vous pas plaint?
23. Ne vous êtes-vous pas écrit?
24. Se sont-elles trompées?
25. S'étaient-ils amusés?

B. Translate.

1. Vous demandez-vous pourquoi il s'est trompé?
2. Comment s'appelait-il?
3. Pourquoi tient-il tant à cette montre?
4. Le professeur tint à parler très fort.
5. Ils s'aimaient tendrement.
6. Les invités venaient de s'asseoir.
7. Ne vous rappelez-vous pas combien le docteur tenait à ses livres?
8. Nous venons d'assister à une cérémonie très impressionante.
9. A quoi cela tient-il?
10. Ils se sont rendus à la Préfecture de Police.
11. Si l'on s'en tient au domaine de la philosophie, cette époque de l'histoire ne vaut pas grand'chose.
12. Les jeunes filles se sont félicitées les unes les autres.
13. Nous venions de nous rencontrer.
14. Rangez-vous le long du mur.
15. J'ai senti que je m'évanouissais.
16. Ailleurs le ciel s'était couvert et il pleuvait comme d'habitude.
17. Nous nous demandions si un accident s'était produit quelque part.
18. Cette décision ne peut s'analyser logiquement.

19. Dans cette nouvelle grammaire on trouve des passages où l'auteur ne tient pas assez compte de l'usage actuel de la langue.

20. A l'issue de la réunion il s'est permis de faire une brève allusion au programme qu'il s'était tracé.

21. Il est resté lui-même à surveiller l'emballage des objets auxquels il tenait le plus.

22. Il est minuit. La dernière lampe du village vient de s'éteindre.

23. Dans cette expérience il s'agit de séparer d'une part l'eau, d'autre part les matières solides.

24. Les microbes se reproduisent à une vitesse vertigineuse.

25. Les électrons sont des particules de très faible masse qui se trouvent autour du noyau.

26. Le noyau d'hydrogène ordinaire s'appelle le proton.

27. Nous allons voir comment s'opère la transformation de la houille en coke.

28. Le principe de l'enregistrement magnétique du son a été découvert avant 1900, mais son application la plus frappante s'est produite assez récemment.

29. En dehors de ces recherches laborieuses, on vient de publier certains articles concernant l'extension de l'enregistrement magnétique à d'autres domaines.

30. Quant à la signalisation ferroviaire, le "block-system" venu des Etats-Unis s'est généralisé chez nous; il vient même d'entrer à l'Académie Française, qui l'a francisé en bloc-système.

C. Drill on the meanings of the verb *être*. Translate.

1. Il est sauvé.
2. Il s'est sauvé.
3. Elle était mariée.
4. Elle s'était mariée.
5. Ils étaient battus.
6. Ils s'étaient battus.
7. Je suis blessée.
8. Je me suis blessée.
9. L'enfant est trouvé.
10. L'enfant s'est trouvé tout seul.
11. La corde était coupée.
12. La corde s'était coupée.
13. Il est retourné.
14. Il s'est retourné.
15. Elle était enfermée dans sa chambre.
16. Elle s'était enfermée dans sa chambre.
17. Il était instruit.
18. Il s'était instruit.
19. La porte est ouverte.
20. La porte s'est ouverte.
21. Nous sommes persuadés qu'il a tort.
22. Nous nous sommes persuadés qu'il avait tort.
23. Ils seraient excusés.
24. Ils se seraient excusés.

D. Translate.

1. You took a walk.
2. Why did you take a walk?
3. Are they fighting?
4. Let's not fight.
5. They had got married.

LESSON V

Devoir; Falloir

REVIEW the parts of the verbs *devoir* and *falloir* in APPENDIX E.

[1]
DEVOIR IN THE MEANING "TO OWE"

The verb *devoir* means "to owe" in all tenses when not followed by an infinitive.

Je lui dois mille francs.	I owe him a thousand francs.
C'est à nous qu'il devait son succès.	It was to us he owed his success.
Si nous lui avions donné l'argent qu'il demandait, il nous aurait dû plus de deux mille dollars.	If we had given him the money he requested, he would have owed us more than two thousand dollars.

[2]
DEVOIR FOLLOWED BY AN INFINITIVE

When the verb *devoir* is followed by an infinitive, it can have four different meanings, each of which is limited to certain tenses and implications.

A] Necessity: "have to," "has to," "must" (present); "had to" (imperfect, past indefinite, past definite); "will have to" (future); and so on. Necessity is expressed by all tenses *except* the conditional and conditional perfect.

Il doit travailler.	He must (has to) work.
Il a dû travailler.	He has had to work. He had to work.
Il devra travailler.	He will have to work.
Il avait dû travailler.	He had had to work.

B] Duty: "ought to," "should" (conditional); "ought to have," "should have" (conditional perfect). Duty is expressed by the conditional and conditional perfect tenses only.

| Il devrait travailler. | He ought to (should) work. |
| Il aurait dû travailler. | He ought to have (should have) worked. |

C] Probability: "must" (present); "must have" (*all* past tenses). Probability is expressed by the present and all past tenses.

Il doit être malade.	He must be sick.
Il a dû être malade.	He must have been sick.
Vous deviez vous demander où elle était.	You must have been wondering where she was.

Present and past indefinite are the two tenses in which this usage most frequently occurs.

D] Futurity: "am to," "is to," "are to" (present); "was to," "were to" (imperfect). The future meaning is expressed by the present and imperfect tenses only.

| Il doit jouer le premier rôle. | He is to play the leading role. |
| Il devait jouer le premier rôle. | He was to play the leading role. |

Devoir, in the future sense, can be translated in some contexts as "is destined to," "is supposed to," "is going to."

[3]
COMMON ERRORS TO BE AVOIDED IN TRANSLATING *DEVOIR*

The various meanings of *devoir* followed by an infinitive give rise to frequent misinterpretation; however, the errors fall mainly into two categories:

A] Failure to restrict the meaning "ought to" (should) and "ought to have" (should have) to the conditional and conditional perfect tenses. The present tense, to be sure, may sometimes have the meaning "ought to," but it should be inferred only when the others clearly do not fit. It should definitely not be considered the routine English equivalent of the present tense.

B] Failure to remember that *devoir* can have the meaning of futurity in the present and imperfect tenses (paragraph 2d). There are sentences in which only this meaning makes sense. The following sentence is a typical example.

Personne ne prévoyait le rôle que le jeune Napoléon devait jouer en France et en Europe.	Nobody foresaw the role that the young Napoleon was to play (was destined to play) in France and in Europe.

[4]
FURTHER OBSERVATIONS ON *DEVOIR*

A] When the form of *devoir* preceding the infinitive is itself an infinitive, the context of the sentence will determine its meaning.

Il croyait devoir nous expliquer sa situation.	He thought he ought to explain his situation to us (had to explain).
Il croyait devoir s'asseoir.	He thought he ought to sit down (had to sit down, was supposed to sit down).

B] Distinguish carefully between *devant*, the present participle of *devoir*, and *devant*, the preposition meaning "before," or "in front of." Note also that the infinitive may be used as a noun: *le devoir*, duty, assignment (particularly in the plural: *devoirs*).

C] "Should" (ought to) translates only the conditional of *devoir*. "Would" is the auxiliary used in English to convey an idea equivalent to the conditional tense of all other French verbs (see Footnote 1, Lesson II).

Il travaillerait plus vite.	He would work faster.
Il devrait travailler plus vite.	He should (ought to) work faster.
Ils croyaient que je partirais plus tôt.	They thought I would leave sooner.
Je devrais partir plus tôt.	I should (ought to) leave sooner.

D] This summary of the meanings of *devoir* does not cover every single use of the verb, but it does offer a plan of attack, and recognition of an occasional variation will come with experience.

[5]
FALLOIR FOLLOWED BY AN INFINITIVE OR CLAUSE

This irregular verb is always used impersonally and therefore exists only in the third person singular (*il faut*).

A] When followed by an infinitive or a clause, *il faut* expresses absolute necessity; the meaning is "must," "it is necessary."

Il faut faire quelque chose.	We must do something. (Something must be done; it is necessary to do something.)
Il faut se taire.	We (you, they, one, people) must keep quiet.
Il faut qu'elle soit là demain.	She must be there tomorrow. (It is necessary that she be there.)
Il faudra qu'il les voie.	He will have to see them.

In the first two examples, in which only an infinitive follows, the idea is general and the subject depends on the context.

In the third and fourth examples, in which a clause follows, the subject of that clause becomes the subject of the English sentence. (NOTE. A clause following *falloir* is in the subjunctive; see Lesson XIII, paragraph 3a.) *Il faut* is impersonal and can never of itself mean "he must," which is expressed by *il faut qu'il...*

B] Although *il faut* can be translated either by "must" or "is necessary," the negative *il ne faut pas* always means "must not."

Il faut y retourner.	You (we, etc.) must return. It is necessary to return.
Il ne faut pas y retourner.	You (we, etc.) must not return.
Il n'est pas nécessaire d'y retourner.	It is not necessary to return.
Il faut qu'il voie cela.	He must see that (it is necessary that he see that).
Il ne faut pas qu'il voie cela.	He must not see that.
Il n'est pas nécessaire qu'il voie cela.	It is not necessary for him to see that.

[6]
FALLOIR FOLLOWED BY A NOUN

When followed by a noun, *il faut* means "it takes" or "is needed," as in the following examples.

Il faut une heure pour y arriver.	It takes an hour to get there.
Il nous faut des tracteurs pour nos fermes.	We need tractors for our farms.

[7]
FURTHER OBSERVATIONS ON *FALLOIR*

A] The imperfect, *il fallait*, is sometimes used in the meaning "you should have" (= *vous auriez dû*).

Vous saviez qu'on vous demandait; il fallait venir tout de suite.	You knew they were asking for you; you should have come immediately.

B] In a reflexive construction, with *en*, *il faut* appears in several idioms that are difficult to translate out of context.

il s'en faut de beaucoup	far from
il s'en faut de peu *peu s'en faut* }	very nearly
tant s'en faut	so far from

EXAMPLES

Il s'en faut de beaucoup que l'affaire soit réglée.	The matter is far from being settled.
Peu s'en est fallu qu'il ne fût écrasé.	He was very nearly run over.

As with *il faut* in general, the subordinate clause in French becomes the main clause in English.

EXERCISES

A. Exercise on *devoir*. If any of the forms in the following sentences can have more than one meaning, give all possible translations.

1. Je dois y retourner à cinq heures.
2. Il devait arriver aujourd'hui, mais il n'est pas encore arrivé.
3. Devons-nous choisir?
4. On nous a dit que nous devions choisir librement.
5. Il a dû s'égarer car il n'est pas revenu.
6. Vous devez vous taire.
7. Vous devrez vous taire.
8. Vous devriez vous taire.
9. Le bureau de poste doit se trouver par ici.
10. Est-ce que j'aurais dû l'aider?
11. A vingt ans il a pris le poste qu'il devait garder pendant toute sa vie.
12. Combien de fois il a dû regretter ses paroles.
13. Mes voisins doivent vendre leur maison.
14. La nouvelle se répandit que trois directeurs de la compagnie devaient quitter leurs fonctions dans les quarante-huit heures.
15. C'est à Oxford que le jeune prince africain apprit ce qu'un personnage royal devait savoir de politique, d'histoire et de science.

16. Une heure plus tard ils étaient à bord de l'avion qui devait les ramener chez eux.
17. A douze ans il a dû quitter l'école et se mettre au travail.
18. En faisant vos comptes vous avez dû commettre quelques erreurs.
19. La conférence me semblait ne devoir jamais finir.
20. Les passagers savaient que, partis à 11 h. 30, ils devaient arriver à 12 h 45.
21. La nouvelle femme de ménage lui a paru si peu satisfaite de ses émoluments qu'il a cru devoir l'augmenter.
22. Cette réaction, pour être sensible, doit être transmise par un appareil amplificateur.
23. Lavoisier imprima à la chimie l'essor qui devait désormais caractériser sa marche.
24. Afin de tenir compte de l'évolution des conditions sociales et de permettre une meilleure utilisation du matériel ferroviaire, l'on a réduit à deux le nombre des classes dans les voitures.
25. C'est à la suite de telles réflexions que l'auteur juge nécessaire de fixer d'abord une méthode pour les recherches à entreprendre et de préciser les époques qui devraient être étudiées.

B. Exercise on *falloir*. Translate.

1. Il faut du courage pour vaincre tout obstacle.
2. Nous faisons ce qu'il faut.
3. Il ne faut pas parler si vite.
4. Il s'en est fallu de peu que Jeanne, qui devait être leur fille la plus illustre, ne mourût dès l'enfance.
5. Il faut que je m'en aille.
6. C'est par là qu'il aurait fallu commencer.
7. Il faut que vous nous aidiez.
8. Il lui faut environ six mois pour écrire un de ses romans policiers.
9. Il fallait lui dire exactement ce que vous pensiez.
10. Il ne faut pas se faire d'illusions sur notre sécurité.

C. Add to the French sentence the word that will complete it in the meaning indicated by the English translation.

1. Il ——————— en accepter la responsabilité.
   He should accept the responsibility for it.
2. Je ——————— écrire mes devoirs.
   I have to write my assignment.
3. Il ——————— faut du pain.
   He needs bread.
4. Ils ——————— être vos guides.
   They are to be your guides.
5. Qu'est-ce qu'il ——————— faire?
   What will he have to do?

LESSON VI

Negatives

[1]
THE PARTICLE *NE*

In French a negative used with a verb normally consists of two parts, one part being the particle *ne* which always precedes the verb.

ne ... pas	not
ne ... point	not
ne ... pas du tout	not at all
ne ... plus	no longer, no more, not any more
ne ... jamais	never
ne ... guère	scarcely
ne ... rien	nothing
ne ... personne	nobody
ne ... aucun (aucune)	no (*adj.*), not a, not one
ne ... nul (nulle)	no (*adj.*), not a, not one
ne ... ni ... ni	neither . . . nor
ne ... que	only

[2]
FRENCH DOUBLE NEGATIVES

In French, negatives may be doubled, tripled, and quadrupled. Translated into cultured English, only one of these negatives will be retained as such; the others will be translated as affirmatives.

Il *n'*en a *jamais rien* dit à *personne*.	He has *never* said *anything* about it to *anyone*.
Je *n'*accepte *plus ni* vos excuses *ni* vos retards.	I *no longer* accept *either* your excuses *or* your delays.

[3]
THE ORDER OF THE PARTS OF THE NEGATIVE

The main part of the negative may precede the *ne*.

Personne n'est venu.	*Nobody* has come.
Rien n'est arrivé.	*Nothing* has happened.
Jamais il *n*'y aurait consenti.	*Never* would he have consented to it.

[4]
NEGATIVES USED WITHOUT A VERB

If there is no verb present, the *ne* is not used.

— Qu'avez-vous apporté?	"What have you brought?"
— Rien.	"Nothing."
Pas d'excuses, s'il vous plaît.	No excuses, please!
Jamais de la vie!	Never! Out of the question!

[5]
NE ... QUE

Ne ... que, "only," is a distinctively French formula requiring the most careful attention. The *que* comes directly before the word modified, which may be well after the verb!

La combinaison *ne* se produit *qu*'entre des volumes égaux d'hydrogène et de chlore.	The combination occurs *only* between equal volumes of hydrogen and chlorine.
On *ne* peut arriver à cette preuve *qu*'en faisant l'expérience précisément comme il l'a faite.	One can arrive at this proof *only* by doing the experiment exactly as he did it (cannot arrive at this proof except by . . .).
Je *ne* vois dans toute cette description interminable *qu*'une franche verbosité.	In all this interminable description I see *only* an out and out verbosity (I see *nothing* in all this interminable description *but*...).

Colloquial American English is quite careless about the placement of "only," but let us say that the *que* in the French sentence is placed where the "only" *ought logically* to be in the English sentence.

[6]
NE ... QUE OCCURRING WITH OTHER NEGATIVES

Ne ... que, when combined with other negatives, has the following meanings:

ne ... plus que	no longer (anything, anybody) except, now only
ne ... jamais que	never (anything, anybody) except
ne ... guère que	scarcely (anything, anybody) except
ne ... rien que	nothing but

EXAMPLES

Cet auteur n'écrit plus que des contes.	This author no longer writes anything but short stories.
Cette coutume n'existe guère plus que chez les Indiens.	This custom scarcely exists any longer except among the Indians.
Je n'ai jamais vu que lui dans le jardin de sa maison.	I have never seen anyone but him in the yard of his house.

Note again here that the *que* does not necessarily follow right after the *plus* or *jamais*, but may come much later in the sentence.

The importance of recognizing this idiom can be seen in the following sentences, in which the addition of the *que* exactly reverses the meaning.

Il ne vient plus nous voir le lundi.	He no longer comes to see us on Mondays.
Il ne vient plus nous voir que le lundi.	He no longer comes to see us except on Mondays.
Ils ne retournent jamais chez eux pour manger.	They never return home to eat.
Ils ne retournent jamais chez eux que pour manger.	They never return home except to eat.

[7]
ADDITIONAL NOTES ON THE VARIOUS NEGATIVES

A] *Jamais* without *ne*, when used with a verb, means "ever." Observe the three uses of *jamais* in the following dialogue.

— Avez-vous jamais vu cet homme auparavant?	"Have you ever seen this man before?"
— Je ne l'ai jamais vu avant aujourd'hui.	"I have never seen him before today."
— Jamais? En êtes-vous sûr?	"Never? Are you sure?"

Jamais also means "ever" in certain idiomatic phrases: *à jamais*, *pour jamais*, forever; *si jamais*, if ever.

B] *Plus* alone appears in the sense "no longer," "no more," chiefly in phrases starting *plus de... .* It is not to be confused with *plus,* "more," as used in comparisons.

Plus de doute!	No more doubt!
— Voulez-vous encore du café?	"Do you want some more coffee?"
— Plus de café, merci.	"No more coffee, thank you."

("More coffee, please" would be *Encore du café, s'il vous plaît.*)

C] *Personne,* used without an article, is the negative "nobody" or "no one" and is masculine. It takes *de* before an adjective. Used with an article (*la personne, une personne, les personnes, des personnes*) it means "person" and is feminine.

Je n'ai vu personne.	I saw no one. (I did not see anyone.)
Je n'ai pas vu la personne dont vous parlez.	I did not see the person of whom you speak.

D] *Rien,* unlike its English equivalent, may come between the auxiliary and the past participle. Also, it takes *de* before an adjective.

Je n'ai rien vu d'extraordinaire.	I saw (have seen) nothing extraordinary.

Rien que, used apart from the verb, means "merely."

Rien qu'en voyant son fauteuil vide, elle fond en larmes.	Merely on seeing his empty chair she breaks into tears.

E] *Pas* may also appear, in what was its original usage, as a masculine noun (*le pas, un pas, les pas, des pas*) meaning "pace" or "step."

F] *Point,* in addition to its use as a negative, may also appear as (1) *le point,* "point," "dot," "period," (2) *point,* the past participle of *poindre,* "to dawn."

G] *Non plus,* "either," is a different type of negative. It is always used in addition to the main negative and apart from the verb. Do not confuse it with *ne ... plus,* which always brackets the verb.

Gabrielle ne vient pas, non plus.	Gabrielle is not coming either.
Gérard, non plus, ne joue jamais au bridge.	Gerard never plays bridge either.

[8]
NEGATIVE WITH INFINITIVE

When an infinitive is negated, the two parts of the negative come together and precede the infinitive.

Je regrette de ne pas aller avec vous.	I am sorry I am not going with you. (I am sorry not to be going with you.)

[9]
NE ALONE AS A NEGATIVE

A] In the case of four verbs, *pouvoir*, *savoir*, *oser*, and *cesser*, the *ne* alone may express the negative (*not*), but even with these verbs the *pas* may appear.

Je ne saurais l'expliquer.	I cannot explain it.
Il n'ose vous le dire.	He does not dare tell you.

B] A negative relative clause takes *ne* alone as "not" if it follows a negative main clause.

Il n'y a aucun savant qui *ne* l'admette.	There is no scientist who does not concede it.

[10]
NE WHEN IT IS NOT NEGATIVE (PLEONASTIC NE)

Sometimes in literary style a *ne* appears alone in a subordinate clause after certain expressions in the main clause. It implies no negation and should be omitted in translation. The reader is most likely to meet it (1) after expressions of fearing (*avoir peur, craindre, de crainte que, de peur que*), (2) after comparisons, (3) after *avant que, à moins que, éviter.* [In (1) and (3) the verb will also be in the subjunctive.]

On craint qu'il ne fasse mal le travail.	They fear that he will do the work poorly.
Je vais me cacher de peur qu'il ne me trouve ici.	I am going to hide for fear that he may find me here.

These clauses become really negative with the addition of a *pas*.

On craint qu'il ne fasse pas le travail.	They are afraid that he will not do the work.
Elle est plus jolie que sa photographie ne le laissait croire.	She is prettier than her picture indicated.
Evitez qu'il ne vous voie.	Avoid letting him see you.

[11]
COMMON ERRORS TO BE AVOIDED IN TRANSLATING FRENCH NEGATIVES

A] With *ne ... que*, a hasty translation of *ne* as "not," followed by confusion as to the meaning of *que*.

SUGGESTIONS

Ne in MAIN CLAUSES can stand alone in the meaning "not" with only four verbs (*pouvoir, savoir, oser, cesser*). With other verbs, if it seems to be alone, there must be another element present—probably *que*!

Ne alone in SUBORDINATE CLAUSES may be ignored, although there is one infrequent exception, mentioned in 9b of this lesson.

B] With compound negatives, including *que* (*ne ... jamais que, ne ... guère que, ne ... plus que, ne ... rien que*), failure to recognize the *que* as also belonging with the *ne* and therefore an interpretation that reverses the writer's meaning.

SUGGESTION

Memorize these four expressions and their meanings.

[12]
IRREGULAR VERBS

Review the parts of the irregular verbs *vivre, dire, lire, battre* in APPENDIX E.

[13]
IDIOMS

dire: to think (in certain expressions appearing in the conditional, conditional perfect, and infinitive)

On dirait qu'il ne s'y intéresse pas.   One would think that he doesn't take an interest in it.

| On aurait dit le cri d'un oiseau blessé. | You would have thought it was the cry of a wounded bird. (It sounded like the cry . . .) |
| Dire que mon propre frère est un voleur! | To think that my own brother is a thief. |

à côté de: beside.

de ce côté: in this direction; on this side.

du côté de: in the direction of, toward.

des deux côtés: on both sides.

de l'autre côté: on the other side.

de mon côté (de leur côté, etc.): for my part (for their part, etc.).

Distinguish *le côté* (side; direction) from *la côte* (coast; slope; rib); *la cote* [quota; assessment; quotation (stock exchange)]. But *côte à côte:* side by side.

EXERCISES

A. Irregular verbs. Identify the tense and translate.

1. Il bat.
2. Il battit.
3. Il se battit.
4. Il ne battit pas.
5. Elle lut.
6. Elle lit.
7. On l'a lue.
8. Ils ne lurent pas.
9. Il dit.
10. Nous dîmes.
11. Se sont-ils battus?
12. Ont-ils battu?
13. Nous nous battions depuis une heure.
14. Il faut que nous nous battions.
15. Ne le disons pas!
16. Ne s'étaient-ils pas battus?
17. Ils dirent.
18. Ils vécurent.
19. Aurait-il vécu?
20. Bien qu'ils vécussent...

B. Drill on negatives. Translate.

1. On ne trouve pas de bêtises dans ce livre.
2. On ne trouve que des bêtises dans ce livre.
3. On ne trouve jamais que des bêtises dans ces livres-là.
4. Personne ne vient ici.
5. Votre client ne vient plus ici.
6. Personne ne vient plus ici.
7. Personne ne vient plus ici que pour bavarder.
8. Mon frère n'aime plus les chats. Ni moi non plus.
9. Vous a-t-il jamais questionné? — Jamais.
10. Il a fait un pas en avant.
11. — Alors, docteur, vous croyez que j'ai la pneumonie?
    — Plus de doute, monsieur.
12. — Qui est à la porte? — Personne.

13. Rien qu'à le voir on devine sa force.
14. Ses deux sœurs vivaient dans la peur qu'il ne les critiquât.
15. Vous n'avez jamais rien trouvé d'intéressant dans cette revue.
16. Ma vieille tante, qui est infirme, ne marche guère qu'appuyée sur sa canne.
17. Cette situation ne semblait guère pouvoir se résoudre qu'au prix de concessions de tous côtés.
18. Charles ne revient plus revoir sa mère.
19. Charles ne revient plus que pour revoir sa mère.
20. Les savants français ne se sont pas intéressés à ces recherches et la publication de volumes étrangers, s'y rapportant, ne semble pas non plus avoir eu en France d'influence immédiate.
21. Un corps ne peut se mouvoir que par rapport à un autre corps choisi comme repère.
22. Adolphe Thiers affirma en 1838 que le chemin de fer ne serait jamais qu'un jouet, alors que déjà fonctionnait la première ligne de St.-Etienne à Lyon et que venait d'être inauguré le premier service de voyageurs entre Paris et St. Germain.
23. L'électrification à 1500 volts des chemins de fer demande des installations qui coûtent cher et ne se justifie que pour des courants de trafic dépassant une certaine importance.
24. Cet ensemble de dispositions techniques dont évidemment nous ne pouvons donner ici qu'un aperçu sommaire n'a pas seulement permis d'assurer un trafic très supérieur en quantité, mais c'est la qualité aussi qui en a bénéficié.
25. On ne pourra déterminer avec exactitude la composition des roches de la Lune que le jour où l'homme aura réussi à en rapporter des échantillons.

C. Translate.

1. Le village où mes cousins habitaient se trouvait de l'autre côté de la rivière.
2. De mon côté, je voulais bien lui donner tout ce qu'il demandait.
3. Personne ne s'est sauvé de ce côté.
4. Et dire qu'il aurait pu se blesser!
5. Il faut tenir compte de toutes ses vertus.

LESSON VII

Causative Faire

[1]
THE BASIC MEANING OF *FAIRE*

In French the verb *faire* expresses ideas which in English are expressed by both "to make" and "to do." In English we "make a noise," "make a dress," "do our duty," "do the work," etc. In French *faire* would be used for all of these.

Elle fait des gâteaux.	She is making some cookies.
Je lui ai demandé ce qu'elle faisait.	I asked him what she was doing.
Georges, qu'avez-vous donc fait?	George, what on earth have you done?

[2]
CAUSATIVE *FAIRE*

A] When followed by an infinitive, the verb *faire* expresses a causal relationship which is variously rendered into English by the verbs "make," "have," "cause," "get." In English we "make somebody do something," "have somebody do something," "have something done," "cause something to be done," etc. In French *faire* is the only verb used in the causative construction.

Il fait travailler les étudiants.	He is making (having) the students work.
La municipalité fait bâtir cent nouvelles maisons.	The municipality is having a hundred new houses built.
Ce traité fit prévaloir la paix pendant vingt ans.	This treaty caused peace to prevail for twenty years
Il s'est fait inviter à la réunion.	He got himself invited to the party.

Notice that in these four examples the simple active infinitive in French always occurs after causative *faire*, which is translated into English by a passive construction in the second and fourth sentences. Other examples are the following:

D'abord il *fera chanter* les élèves.	First he *will have* the pupils *sing*.
D'abord il *fera chanter* une chanson.	First he *will have* a song *sung*.

B] In French construction the infinitive forms an essentially inseparable unit with *faire*. Noun objects follow the whole unit; pronoun objects precede it. Note how they contrast with English in the following sentences.

Il *fait travailler* les étudiants.	He *makes* the students *work*.
Il les *fait travailler*.	He *makes* them *work*.
Il *fait étudier* la leçon.	He *has* the lesson *studied*.
Il *fait étudier* la leçon aux étudiants.	He *has* the students *study* the lesson.
Il la leur *fait étudier*.	He *has* them *study* it.
Il leur *fait étudier* la leçon.	He *has* them *study* the lesson.

In the last three examples it can be seen that if both *faire* and the infinitive have objects the object of *faire* will appear in the indirect form. An additional example of this construction is the following:

C'est ce critique qui a fait apprécier notre poète aux générations suivantes.	It was this critic who caused later generations to appreciate our poet (caused our poet to be appreciated by later generations).

SUGGESTIONS FOR TRANSLATION:

(1) If an indirect object is present in the causative *faire* construction, place its English equivalent immediately after the translation of *faire*.

(2) If the causative *faire* occurs in a long sentence or with confusing new vocabulary, the best meaning to try first is usually "cause." Though perhaps awkward, it will point toward the right meaning.

Si vous allez trop près des ruches, vous allez vous faire piquer.	If you go too close to the hives (you are going to cause yourself to be stung) you are going to get stung.

C] In a few cases the combination of *faire* and the infinitive can be considered an idiom, equivalent to a single English verb.

faire voir	to show	*faire savoir*	to inform
faire entrer	to show in	*faire remarquer*	to point out
faire venir	to send for		

EXAMPLES

Allez-vous faire venir le médecin?	Are you going to send for the doctor?
Faites-moi voir le livre dont vous parlez.	Show me the book you are talking about.

These idioms show the meaning of *faire* as greatly weakened.

[3]
OTHER VERBS LIKE CAUSATIVE *FAIRE*

Laisser, "to let," "allow," and the verbs that express sense perception (*entendre, voir*), may take the same construction as *faire*.

J'aime ses petites chansons. Laissez-les-lui chanter.	I like her little songs. Let her sing them.
Il a vu tuer le brigand.	He saw the brigand killed.

Note: Le fait, "fact," is not to be confused with the parts of *faire*.

[4]
IRREGULAR VERBS

Review the irregular verbs (1) *faire*, (2) *partir* and all verbs like it, notably *sortir, servir, dormir, sentir, mentir,* and *consentir,* in APPENDIX E.

[5]
IDIOMS

il fait (impersonal); with expressions indicating the weather.

Il fait beau (mauvais).	It is fine (bad) weather.
Il fait du vent (de la pluie).	It is windy (rainy).
Il fait déjà nuit.	It is already night. (It is already dark.)

faire mal à: to hurt.

Mon doigt me fait mal.	My finger is hurting me.

faire du bien (mal) à: to do good (harm) to.

Un voyage vous fera du bien à tous.	A trip will do you all good.

faire le malade, le généreux: to pretend illness, generosity (to try to appear rich, generous).

Ma chère amie, vous avez fait la malade assez longtemps.	My dear friend, you have pretended to be ill long enough.

fit-il implies *dit-il*, frequently in formal style.

Moi non, fit-il.	"Not I," he said.

se faire: to get, become, make oneself; to form; to happen, come about.

Il se fait tard. (impersonal)	It is getting late.
Elle se faisait vieille.	She was getting old.
Jacques se fit prêtre.	James became a priest.
Maurice s'est fait une idée très étrange des Américains.	Maurice has formed a very strange idea of the Americans. (*Literally*, "has made for himself"; here *se* is an indirect object.)
Comment se fait-il que vous soyez ici?	How does it happen that you are here?

se faire is sometimes simply a substitute for the passive voice (see Lesson 4, paragraph 1c):

Ces choses ne se font pas.	Those things are not done.

se faire à: to get accustomed to.

A la longue on se fait à tout.	In the long run you get used to anything.

Cela ne fait rien: That makes no difference.

— Qu'est-ce que cela vous fait?	What difference does that make to you?
— Cela ne me fait rien.	That makes no difference to me.

ne faire que: only, just (to do nothing but).

Il ne faisait que sourire.	He only smiled. (He would only smile.)

se servir de: to use (= *employer, user de*).

— Voulez-vous vous servir de mon livre?	"Do you want to use my book?"
— Je m'en sers déjà.	"I am already using it."

servir de: to serve as.

Qui va nous servir d'interprète?	Who is going to serve as our interpreter?

servir à: to be useful (for something, for doing something).

A quoi cela sert-il?	What is the use of that?

EXERCISES

A. Irregular verbs. Identify the tense and translate.

1. Il sert.	11. Ils partirent.
2. Il servait.	12. Ils ne consentirent pas.
3. Il servit.	13. Ils consentent.
4. Servira-t-il?	14. Ils consentiront.
5. Servirait-il?	15. On ment.
6. Je veux que tu t'en serves.	16. On mentit.
7. Nous nous en étions servis.	17. Sont-elles sorties?
8. Dort-il?	18. Ils feraient.
9. Il se peut qu'il dorme.	19. Il ne faut pas qu'ils le fassent.
10. Ils partent.	20. Ils font.

B. Translate.

1. Ses arguments ont beaucoup fait pour me convaincre.
2. Les enfants faisaient beaucoup de bruit.
3. Il fait la cuisine pour tous.
4. Mon oncle bâtit une maisonette sur cette colline.
5. Mon oncle fait bâtir une maison.
6. Mon oncle a fait bâtir une maison.
7. Il s'est fait bâtir une maison.
8. Elle se fait une robe.
9. Elle se fait faire une robe.
10. Elle s'est fait faire une robe.
11. Le patron fait soigner les jeunes arbres par les jardiniers.
12. Il les leur fait soigner.
13. Charles fait bien son travail.
14. Charles fait bien faire le travail.
15. Il le leur fait bien faire.
16. Le professeur leur faisait prononcer les mots plus lentement.
17. Il les leur faisait prononcer.
18. Faites manger le pain aux enfants.
19. Cette catastrophe fit oublier les événements de la veille.
20. Au bout d'un certain temps, sa mère se fit à cette nouvelle vie.
21. Elle s'y fit lentement.
22. Les yeux me font mal.
23. L'étude d'une langue étrangère devrait faire apprécier aux étudiants la civilisation du pays où on la parle.
24. Le résultat ne se fit pas attendre.

25. Marseille ressemblait peu à l'idée que nous nous en étions faite.
26. Quand mon grand-père ne veut pas répondre à une question, il fait le sourd.
27. Puisqu'il fait beau, un voyage ferait du bien à tout le monde.
28. Qu'est-ce que cela leur fait?
29. Nos voisins se font difficiles.
30. C'est un roi de nom plutôt que de fait.
31. Ne vous livrez pas tout de suite. Laissez-lui faire le premier pas.
32. Il est fâcheux qu'on lui fasse jouer un rôle qui n'est pas le sien.
33. Cette famille pourrait servir d'exemple, d'illustration à la thèse que je viens d'exposer.
34. Il fit faire à ses frais des expériences au sujet de la composition du sol de sa région.
35. Si on porte le liquide à ébullition, on peut, par la suite, lui laisser subir toutes les variations de température des saisons sans qu'il éprouve aucune altération.

C. Translate into French.

1. He is making each student read a paragraph.
2. He is making him read it.
3. Have you heard his car go out?
4. His secretary showed them in.
5. You have done enough.

VOCABULARY SUGGESTIONS

1. chaque l'étudiant le paragraphe   4. la secrétaire
2. lire   5. assez
3. entendre la voiture sortir

LESSON VIII

Nouns and Adjectives

[1]
PLURAL OF NOUNS AND ADJECTIVES

NOUNS for the most part form their plurals in -s, as in English (but the -s is usually not pronounced). Most French adjectives also form their plurals in -s. Other ways, however, are reviewed here.

A] Sometimes the plural is formed by adding -x.

SING.		PLURAL
la peau	(*skin*)	les peaux
le feu	(*fire*)	les feux
le chou	(*cabbage*)	les choux
beau	(*beautiful*)	beaux

B] If the singular forms already end in -s, -x, or -z, there is no change in the plural.

SING.		PLURAL
le fils	(*son*)	les fils
le nez	(*nose*)	les nez
l'index	(*index*)	les index
épais	(*thick*)	épais

C] The plural ending **-aux** deserves special attention because it disguises the singular form. Most nouns and adjectives ending in **-al** in the singular form their plural in **-aux**. A few nouns in **-ail** do the same.

SING.		PLURAL
l'animal	(*animal*)	les animaux
le mal	(*evil, pain*)	les maux
le journal	(*newspaper*)	les journaux
spécial		spéciaux
national		nationaux

(Feminine singular and plural forms are regular: *spéciale,
spéciales,* etc.)

SING.		PLURAL
le travail	(*work*)	les travaux
l'émail	(*enamel*)	les émaux
le vitrail	(*stained glass window*)	les vitraux

D] The following irregular plurals should be memorized.

SING.		PLURAL
l'œil	(*eye*)	les yeux
le ciel	(*heaven, sky*)	les cieux

E] Proper nouns in French, in contrast to the English, do not
add an **-s** to form the plural. They depend entirely on the article
to show plurality.

Les Dupont parlent français aux　　The Duponts speak French to the
　Smith.　　　　　　　　　　　　　　Smiths.

[2]
IRREGULAR FEMININE FORMS OF ADJECTIVES

A] A number of French adjectives have irregular feminine
forms, but often the irregularity is so slight that the root form is
easily recognized: *bas, basse; cher, chère.* Others require more
study to be identified correctly. Note the following:

MASC.	FEM.	
blanc	blanche	(*white*)
doux	douce	(*sweet, gentle*)
faux	fausse	(*false*)
frais	fraîche	(*cool, fresh*)
long	longue	(*long*)
sec	sèche	(*dry*)

B] In addition to these individual cases, a large group of
adjectives ending in **-eux** in the masculine take **-euse** in the
feminine.

EXAMPLES

MASC. SING.	FEM. SING.	MASC. PLURAL	FEM. PLURAL	
cérémonieux	cérémonieuse	cérémonieux	cérémonieuses	(*ceremonious*)
heureux	heureuse	heureux	heureuses	(*happy*)
prodigieux	prodigieuse	prodigieux	prodigieuses	(*prodigious*)

C] Five French adjectives not only have an irregular feminine form but also an extra form in the masculine singular for use before a vowel or a mute **h**.

MASC. SING.	FEM. SING.	MASC. PLURAL	FEM. PLURAL	
beau, bel	belle	beaux	belles	(*beautiful, fine*)
fou, fol	folle	fous	folles	(*crazy*)
mou, mol	molle	mous	molles	(*soft*)
nouveau, nouvel	nouvelle	nouveaux	nouvelles	(*new*)
vieux, vieil	vieille	vieux	vieilles	(*old*)

The second masculine singular form is pronounced just like the feminine.

[3]
ADJECTIVES USED AS NOUNS

A very important difference between the French adjective and the English is that in French any adjective may be used as a personal noun merely by the addition of an article.

EXAMPLES

malade (adj.): sick.

le malade	the sick man, the sick boy, the patient
la malade	the sick woman, the sick girl, the patient

Distinguish between *le malade, la malade,* "patient," and *la maladie,* "sickness."

mort, morte (adj.): dead.

le mort	the dead man (boy)
la morte	the dead woman (girl) (BUT: *la mort,* death)
le riche	the rich man
les riches	the rich people, the rich
la vieille	the old woman

Since the English article does not express gender, the words "man" or "woman" ("boy" or "girl") must be added to obtain the English equivalent of a singular French adjective used as a noun. Note, however, that English does use the adjective alone with the article in a plural sense; "the rich," "the blind," "the unfortunate" would be a correct translation only of *les riches, les aveugles, les misérables* (not of *le riche, l'aveugle, le misérable*).

[4]
WORD ORDER OF NOUN AND ADJECTIVE

A] In French most *descriptive* adjectives come after the noun, in contrast to English, in which adjectives of all types regularly come before the noun.[1]

les actions mécaniques réciproques	the reciprocal mechanical actions
un philosophe existentialiste	an existentialist philosopher
ce fait sociologique fondamental	this fundamental sociological fact

B] The following common descriptive adjectives regularly precede the noun: *bon, mauvais, grand, petit, gros, jeune, nouveau, vieux, long, court, beau, joli, cher.*

un jeune homme	a young man
le nouvel hôtel	the new hotel

C] Some adjectives change meaning according to their placement—whether before or after the noun. Five typical examples, probably the most frequently occurring in this group, are the following:

l'ancien sénateur	the former senator
l'histoire ancienne	ancient history
la même chose	the same thing
la chose même	the very thing, the thing itself
un verre propre	a clean glass
mon propre verre	my own glass
un homme brave	a brave man
de braves gens	fine people
neuf livres	nine books
un livre neuf	a new book

Neuf, when it precedes the noun, is the numeral "nine" and is invariable: when it follows the noun, it means "new" and makes the usual agreement (*neuf, neuve, neufs, neuves*).

Même has an additional use as an adverb meaning "even":

Il a même refusé.   He has even refused.

---

[1] Even in English the adjective may follow the noun if the adjective has a dependent phrase; so *un mot difficile à définir* would be "a word difficult to define."

Sometimes, for emphasis or other stylistic reasons, a descriptive adjective may be taken out of its usual position and may precede the noun.

une excellente idée	an excellent idea
la principale cause	the principal cause
de patientes recherches	some patient research

In such cases the noun is easily identified because it is distinctive in form from any adjective.

D] A point of frequent confusion is found in the noun-adjective group in which, according to mere form, one or both words could be either an adjective or a noun. Assume here that the basic word order is being followed (in other words, that the first word is the noun).[2]

le critique étranger	the foreign critic
cet étranger distingué	this distinguished foreigner
la moyenne étrangère	the foreign average
un historique fort intéressant	a very interesting historical account
un fort historique très intéressant	a very interesting historical fort
la même belle politique étrangère	the same fine foreign policy

Study the following common words which can be used either as nouns or adjectives and therefore depend on their positions to show their meaning.

le critique	critic
la critique	criticism
critique (adj.)	critical
le moyen	means
la moyenne	average
moyen, -ne (adj.)	average
la politique	policy, politics
politique (adj.)	political
le sommaire	summary, synopsis
sommaire (adj.)	summary, concise
la rose	rose (flower)
rose (adj.)	pink

---

[2] What misleads those reading French is that in English the noun in such a series is always the *last word*: a Venetian blind, a blind Venetian, a house dog, a dog house, a patient woman, a woman patient.

l'industriel	manufacturer
industriel, -elle (*adj.*)	industrial
le savant	scholar, scientist
savant, -e (*adj.*)	learned
la caractéristique	characteristic
caractéristique (*adj.*)	characteristic
la technique	technique, technology
technique (*adj.*)	technical
le particulier	individual
particulier, -ière (*adj.*)	private, peculiar
la pratique	practice
pratique (*adj.*)	practical
l'étranger	foreigner
l'étrangère (*f.*)	foreigner, foreign woman
étranger, -ère (*adj.*)	foreign
l'ouvrier	worker, working man
l'ouvrière	female worker, working woman
ouvrier, -ère (*adj.*)	working (that is, pertaining to workers)
l'historique	historical account, chronological account
historique (*adj.*)	historical, historic

[5]
AGREEMENT OF ADJECTIVE WITH NOUN

The agreement of the adjective with the noun usually presents no difficulty. Note, however, the following case:

l'architecture et la musique françaises.	French architecture and music.
l'architecture et l'art français (américains).	French (American) architecture and art.

The adjectives are plural because they qualify both singular nouns. This is shown in English by putting the adjective before them. *Françaises* is feminine plural because it modifies two feminine singular nouns. *Français* and *américains* modify one masculine singular and one feminine singular noun, and are therefore in the masculine plural.

[6]
COMPARISON OF ADJECTIVES

The French adjective is compared as follows:

petit	plus petit	le plus petit
(*small*)	(*smaller*)	(*the smallest*)
	moins petit	le moins petit
	(*less small*)	(*the least small*)
heureuse	plus heureuse	la plus heureuse
(*happy*)	(*happier*)	(*the happiest*)
beaux	plus beaux	les plus beaux
(*beautiful*)	(*more beautiful*)	(*the most beautiful*)

IRREGULAR

bon	meilleur	le meilleur
(*good*)	(*better*)	(*the best*)

Ce fut la plus longue journée de sa vie.	It was the longest day of his life.
Hélène est la jeune fille la plus heureuse que je connaisse.	Helen is the happiest girl I know.
On a donné le prix au plus rapide.	They gave the prize to the fastest one.

A] The addition of the definite article *or* a possessive adjective to the comparative form of a French adjective raises it to the superlative.

Les meilleures compositions sont très courtes.	The best compositions are very short.
Ses meilleures compositions sont très courtes.	His best compositions are very short.

B] In the following illustration French uses the superlative even if there is a question of only two. Cultured English does not permit this form.

De ses deux filles laquelle est la plus jolie?	Of his two daughters which is the prettier?

C] Note the following idiomatic use of the superlative.

C'est un conférencier des plus distingués.	He is a most distinguished lecturer.
Il a mentionné une affaire des plus délicates.	He mentioned a most delicate matter.

D] A comparison of equality is shown by *aussi* + adjective or adverb + *que*, "as . . . as."

Les microbes meurent aussi vite   Microbes die as fast as they are
qu'ils naissent.   born.

Sometimes this usage is elliptical, the comparison stopping at the adjective.

Le sol s'adapte très bien à la vini-   The soil is very well adapted to
culture. Le climat est tout aussi   viniculture. The climate is just as
favorable.   favorable.

[7]
IRREGULAR VERBS

Study the irregular verb *ouvrir* and the other verbs with similar characteristics (*couvrir, souffrir, offrir*) in APPENDIX E.

[8]
IDIOMS

la nouvelle: news.
une nouvelle: an item of news.
ses nouvelles: news of him.
mes nouvelles: news of me.

Avez-vous reçu de ses nouvelles?   Have you received any news of
                                       him?

avoir beau (+ *inf.*): to find it useless (to do something).

This idiom can scarcely be translated out of context. It is often equivalent to a clause in English beginning "although," "no matter how (what)," "it is useless," or a similar expression.

J'ai beau vous parler, vous n'écou-   It is useless for me to talk to you
tez pas.   (no matter what I say to you),
                                         you do not listen.

Il a eu beau lutter, il n'a pas pu   Although he struggled (no matter
échapper à son sort.   how hard he struggled, in spite
                                         of his struggles), he could not
                                         escape his fate.

sur le compte de: about . . . .

sur mon compte, sur votre compte: about me, about you.

— Qu'avez-vous entendu sur mon   What have you heard about me?
compte?

— Rien. Mais j'ai appris quelque   Nothing. But I learned something
chose sur le compte du meunier.   about the miller.

se rendre compte de (que): to realize.

Je me suis rendu compte qu'il avait   I realized that he had achieved his
réalisé son but.   goal.

See also *tenir compte de,* Lesson IV.

EXERCISES

A. Irregular verbs. Identify the tense and translate.

1. Il ouvre.	11. Ils ouvraient.
2. Il ouvrit.	12. Ils ouvriraient.
3. Il a ouvert.	13. Ils ouvrirent.
4. Elle souffre.	14. Ils souffrirent.
5. Elle souffrit.	15. Ils souffriront.
6. Couvre-t-il?	16. Ils furent découverts.
7. Couvrit-il?	17. Ils sont couverts.
8. On offrait.	18. Ils se sont couverts.
9. On offrirait.	19. Nous souffrions.
10. On offrira.	20. Nous souffririons.

B. Irregular adjectives.

I. Name the masculine singular form of each of the following
adjectives. If there is no obvious cognate in English, translate.

principaux	médicaux	phénoménaux	capitaux	rivaux
moraux	mondiaux	monumentaux	estivaux	continentaux
filiaux	sentimentaux	loyaux	vitaux	amicaux
végétaux	cristaux	longitudinaux	spatiaux	latéraux

II. Write out and pronounce the masculine singular form of each
of the following adjectives. Translate.

prodigieuse	complète	gentille	fausse
merveilleuse	sèche	cruelles	blanche
heureuses	légère	folles	épaisse
gracieuses	fraîche	vieille	longues
belliqueuse	douces	molle	

III. Noun-adjective word order. Translate.

1. une rose moyenne	3. les organisations ouvrières
2. une robe rose	4. les ouvrières organisées

5. un fort historique
6. un historique fort amusant
7. une critique sommaire
8. le point critique
9. les ouvrières étrangères
10. le Français moyen
11. la belle et jeune étrangère
12. des savants français
13. un Français savant
14. le potentiel industriel
15. neuf industriels étrangers
16. une politique toute neuve
17. le revenu moyen

18. un moyen légitime
19. la moyenne politique
20. la politique moyenne
21. la politique même
22. le même moyen politique
23. la politique caractéristique
24. les caractéristiques politiques
25. des religieuses françaises
26. une affaire religieuse
27. les malades étrangers
28. les étrangères malades
29. une politique pratique
30. une pratique politique

C. Idiomatic sentences. Translate.

1. Les Curie découvrirent la radioactivité.
2. Un muet est toujours sourd, mais un sourd n'est pas toujours muet.
3. Le médecin regardait attentivement sa malade. Il était un peu gêné de ne pouvoir se prononcer sur la nature de la maladie dont elle souffrait.
4. Je viens de faire la connaissance de la jolie petite Johnson, l'amie de la petite Boulanger.
5. Quand j'ai vu ces deux jeunes garçons tout à l'heure, le grand aidait le petit.
6. Raoul, cet impatient, s'est servi d'un moyen caractéristique pour nous envoyer de ses nouvelles.
7. Ils croyaient que je divaguais, mais je n'ai jamais été aussi raisonnable.
8. Alice Duvivier, ancien mannequin, est maintenant mère de deux enfants.
9. L'avocat a répondu au juge en donnant une explication des plus habiles.
10. La Belgique a une population très dense; aucun autre pays d'Europe n'a tant d'habitants sur un territoire aussi restreint.
11. Ces impôts pèsent aussi lourdement sur l'ouvrier que sur le riche.
12. En ayant recours à des moyens techniques, ils ont beaucoup allégé le travail.
13. On eut beau dire, il ne voulut pas céder.
14. J'ai entendu sur son compte des choses fort étranges, mais qui peuvent être fausses.
15. On a couvert d'une substance molle la surface blanche et sèche.
16. Nous étudions les volumes monumentaux qu'il a écrits sur la chute des Bonaparte.
17. Une scène des plus bizarres s'est offerte à nos yeux.
18. A force d'approfondir ces différentes branches de la science, on s'est rendu compte qu'elles demandaient toutes une connaissance de la structure de la matière.
19. La durée moyenne de l'incubation chez les animaux inoculés est de 15 jours environ.
20. Cette initiative a largement contribué à développer l'introduction de ces nouvelles méthodes de travail dans les domaines les plus divers de la recherche en Europe.
21. Nous avons déjà rappelé les plus importantes réussites des expériences depuis l'automne de 1960 jusqu'à la fin de 1962.

22. Alors Ampère proposa son hypothèse, des plus hardies à l'époque, de l'aimantation.

23. Beaucoup de métaux se rencontrent dans la nature unis au soufre.

24. Il ne s'agit ici ni d'un ouvrage de botanique ni d'un ouvrage de zoologie. L'auteur tient avant tout à éveiller la curiosité des jeunes en leur montrant les plus prodigieux spectacles de la création.

25. Les sujets dont les cas sont traités dans ce rapport médical sont des malades mentaux du sexe masculin.

Personal Pronouns; Y and EN

[1]
PERSONAL PRONOUNS

A] Personal pronouns in French are described as conjunctive and disjunctive. Conjunctive pronouns are those normally used as subject, object, or indirect object of the verb. The disjunctive pronouns are those used apart from the verb (object of preposition, etc.) or to show emphasis. The complete list is given here to permit a quick review.

	Conjunctive						Disjunctive	
SUBJECT		OBJECT		INDIRECT OBJECT				
je	*(I)*	me	*(me)*	me	*(to me)*		moi	*(I, me)*
tu	*(you)*	te	*(you)*	te	*(to you)*		toi	*(you)*
il	*(he, it)*	le	*(him, it)*	lui	*(to him)*		lui	*(he, him)*
elle	*(she, it)*	la	*(her, it)*	lui	*(to her)*		elle	*(she, her)*
nous	*(we)*	nous	*(us)*	nous	*(to us)*		nous	*(we, us)*
vous	*(you)*	vous	*(you)*	vous	*(to you)*		vous	*(you)*
ils	*(they)*	les	*(them)*	leur	*(to them)*		eux	*(they, them)*
elles	*(they)*	les	*(them)*	leur	*(to them)*		elles	*(they, them)*

B] Most of the French pronouns are easily understood; however, two uses of the disjunctive should be carefully noted.

(1) The disjunctive *lui* as an emphatic form replacing *il*.

Elle est très instruite; *lui* ne sait   She is very well educated; *he* can
guère écrire son propre nom.   scarcely write his own name.

(2) The use of a disjunctive to reduplicate a pronoun or a noun in order to emphasize it.

Moi, je pense que vous avez tort.   *I* think you are wrong.
Tu ne fais rien, *toi*!   *You* don't do anything!
Ses *amis* ont protesté, *eux aussi*,   His *friends*, *also*, protested that he
qu'il était trop sévère.   was too strict.

The equivalent effect is obtained in English by stressing with the voice when reading orally, by underscoring or using distinctive type when writing or printing.

Note also that *lui* as a conjunctive indirect object can be either masculine or feminine ("to him," "to her,"), whereas the disjunctive *lui* is exclusively masculine ("he," "him").

— Pourquoi Charles n'a-t-il pas aimé ces livres?	"Why didn't Charles like these books?"
— Oh! Mais je ne les *lui* ai pas montrés à *lui*; je les ai montrés à Yvonne.	"Oh! I didn't show them *to him*; I showed them to Yvonne."
— Qui fait ce bruit?	"Who is making that noise?"
— Lui.	"He is."

C] The masculine pronoun *le* is used as a neuter particle in the predicate to replace an adjective or a noun which has already been mentioned.

Robert est grand; Jean *l'*est aussi.	Robert is tall; John is, too.
Il suffit de faire bouillir ce mélange pour séparer l'alcool, plus volatile, de l'eau qui *l'*est moins.	It is sufficient to boil this mixture to separate the alcohol, which is more volatile, from the water, which is less *so*.

In English these words are understood after their first mention or are sometimes replaced by "so."

The reverse is true in the following sentences, in which French does not use a pronoun but English does.

Il a jugé prudent de s'absenter.	He judged *it* advisable to stay away.
On a trouvé utile de ralentir la marche de la machine.	They found *it* useful to slow down the operation of the machine.

[2]
THE ADVERBIAL PRONOUNS *Y* AND *EN*

English has many little prepositional phrases such as "from it," "from them," "about it," "to it," and "in it," which are lacking in French and are replaced chiefly by the adverbial pronouns *en* and *y* when referring to objects.

A] *En* is a pronoun that replaces *de* + a noun. *De* can have a great many meanings and *en* takes on all of them.

(1) *En* can be used as a partitive pronoun, meaning "some," or with a numeral or an adverb of quantity in the meaning "of it" or "of them."

Il a des livres.	He has some books.
Il en a.	He has some.
(*En= des livres*).	
Combien de livres avez-vous?	How many books have you?
J'en ai trois.	I have three (of them).
(*En= des livres*).	
J'ai de l'argent, mais je n'en ai pas beaucoup.	I have some money, but not a lot (of it).
(*En= d'argent*).	

(2) *De* is also a preposition meaning "of," "from," or "about." Accordingly, *en* may mean "of it (them)," "from it (them)," or "about it (them)."

Ils parlent du beau temps.	They are talking about the fine weather.
Ils en parlent.	They are talking about it.
Les uns vont au travail; les autres en reviennent.	Some are going to work; others are returning from it.
Les uns vont aux mines; les autres en reviennent.	Some are going to the mines; others are returning from them.

(3) *De* is used in a number of idioms, whose English equivalents employ a variety of prepositions or none at all, and *en* reflects all these possibilities. As examples, note the following idiomatic expressions which contain first a noun object, then a pronoun object.

couvert de	covered with
se passer de	to do without
douter de	to doubt
se souvenir de	to remember

Le toit est couvert *de pigeons*.	The roof is covered *with pigeons*.
Le toit *en* est couvert.	The roof is covered *with them*.
Il se passe *de loupe*.	He is getting along *without the magnifying glass*.
Il s'*en* passe.	He is getting along *without it*.
— Doutez-vous *de sa sincérité*?	"Do you doubt *his sincerity*?"
— Oui, j'*en* doute.	"Yes, I doubt *it*."
Je me souviendrai *de ses dernières paroles*.	I will remember *his last words*.
Je m'*en* souviendrai toujours.	I will remember *them* forever.

Whenever an idiomatic expression includes *de*, it takes *en* when its object is a pronoun referring to a thing.

(4) Note the following further possibilities of *en* as a pronoun.

En parlant de l'Alaska, on n'*en* souligne pas assez l'énorme étendue.	In talking about Alaska, people do not sufficiently emphasize *its* enormous size.
J'aime les vieux arbres. Il y *en* a de très vieux dans mon jardin.	I love old trees. There are *some* very old *ones* in my garden.
Il vient de Paris. Il *en* vient.	He comes from Paris. He comes *from there*.
Le professeur Duval a lu plusieurs mémoires devant l'Institut de Physique; il *en* est devenu assez connu.	Professor Duval has read several scientific papers before the Institute of Physics; *because of this* he has become rather well known.

The last example differs from all the others cited in that *en* replaces a whole clause, not just a phrase beginning with *de*.

B] *Y* as a pronoun replaces a phrase beginning with *à, dans, sur*, or certain other prepositions, but never *de*.

— Le papier est *dans le tiroir*.	"The paper is *in the drawer*."
— Je ne l'*y* ai pas vu.	"I did not see it *there*."
— J'ai laissé mon livre *sur le bureau*, n'est-ce pas?	"I left my book *on the desk*, didn't I?"
— Non, vous n'*y* avez rien laissé.	"No, you did not leave anything *on it* (*there*)."
Je pense à mon travail très souvent. En effet, j'*y* pense trop souvent.	I think *about my work* very often. In fact, I think *about it* too often.
Il est entré *dans le salon*. Il *y* est entré sans hésiter.	He entered *the living room*. He entered *it* without hesitating.
Il a répondu *à ma lettre*. Il *y* a répondu hier.	He answered *my letter*. He answered *it* yesterday.

Notice that in the last two examples the *y* is translated as "it" because the idiomatic *entrer dans* and *répondre à* can be represented by English verbs that are not followed by prepositions: "enter" and "answer." (They can, of course, also be translated by "go into" and "reply to.")

C] It frequently happens that the reader of French cannot identify an idiom that he encounters in the text because he has failed to find the *de* or *à* which the expression displays in an idiom list or textbook vocabulary. It must be remembered that the *de* or *à* appears only when the object of the idiom is a *noun*; when the object is a *pronoun*, the preposition is usually absorbed into the words *en* (in case of *de*), *y* or *lui* (*leur*) (in case of *à* or certain other prepositions).

se servir de: to use.

Il se sert *du bateau.*	He is using the boat.
Il s'*en* sert.	He is using it.

obéir à: to obey.

Il obéit *à mes ordres.*	He obeys my orders.
Il *y* obéit.	He obeys them.
Il obéit *à son père.*	He obeys his father.
Il *lui* obéit.	He obeys him.

D] Do not confuse the pronoun *en*, whose meanings are given in the preceding paragraphs, with the preposition *en*.

(1) Some of the commonest meanings of *en* as a preposition are as follows:

en France, en Europe	in (to) France, in (to) Europe
en été, en hiver	in summer, in winter
en l'honneur de	in honor of
en parlant	while (by) speaking (see Lesson III, paragraph 2)

PREPOSITION AND PRONOUN IN JUXTAPOSITION

Vous trouverez la source de cette rivière *en en* suivant les sinuosités.	You will find the source of this stream *by* following *its* windings.

(2) *En* means "like a" or "as a" in the following usage:

St.-Guillaume, en bon village méridional, s'étire sur la montagne aride.	St. Guillaume, like a good southern village, stretches out over the arid mountain.

[3]
IRREGULAR VERBS

Study the principal parts of the irregular verb *craindre* and the verbs that are similarly conjugated (*plaindre, atteindre, éteindre, feindre, peindre, joindre*) in APPENDIX E.

[4]
IDIOMS

Sometimes an idiom will contain an *en* or an *y* that does not refer to anything previously mentioned. Note particularly the following:

s'en aller: to go away.
s'en prendre à: to blame.
s'en tenir à: to stick to (see Lesson IV, paragraph 8).
en vouloir à: to bear a grudge against (see Lesson II, paragraph 8).
peu s'en faut: very nearly (see Lesson V, paragraph 7b).
il y a: there is, there are.
s'y prendre: to go about it.
en être à: to be as far along as.

Où en sommes-nous?	Where are we? (How far along are we?)
Nous en sommes à la page 9.	We are on page 9.

Study the next groups, noting carefully the basic meaning of the verb and the alteration caused in the meaning by the addition of a reflexive pronoun, a preposition, or both. Some of these idioms have been presented in preceding lessons. All can bear further study in a dictionary.

servir: to serve, to be useful.
servir à: to be useful for (something, for doing something).
servir de (+noun): to serve as.
se servir de: to use (see Lesson VII).

attendre: to wait for.
s'attendre à: to expect.

passer: to pass; to spend (for example, *passer du temps*).
se passer: to take place (=*avoir lieu, arriver, se produire*).
se passer de: to do without.

douter de: to doubt.
se douter de: (*se douter que*) to suspect (=*soupçonner*).

plaindre: to pity.
se plaindre de: to complain about.

garder: to keep.

se garder de: to be careful not to (do something).

disposer: to arrange.

disposer de: to have at one's disposal, to have available.

tenir: to hold.

tenir à: to be very fond of; to insist upon; to be due to.

tenir de: to take after.

EXERCISES

A. *Irregular verbs.* Identify the tense and translate.

1. Il craint.
2. Il a craint.
3. Il craignait.
4. Il craignit.
5. Il peint.
6. Il a peint.
7. Il peignait.
8. Il peignit.
9. Il est peint.
10. Elle joint.
11. Elle a joint.
12. Elle joignit.
13. Feignant.
14. Ils feignent.
15. Nous plaignons.
16. Nous nous en sommes plaints.
17. Il faut qu'on peigne.
18. Il éteint.
19. Il est éteint.
20. Il s'est éteint.

B. Translate.

1. Il s'attendait à voir apparaître le directeur de l'école.
2. Il s'y attendait.
3. — Voici ma machine à écrire. Servez-vous-en!
   — Merci. Je vais m'en servir.
4. Il ne faut pas vous en prendre à Georges. Pourquoi lui en voulez-vous?
5. — Regardez cette maison. Le toit est couvert de pigeons. Comment dois-je m'y prendre pour m'en débarrasser?
6. — C'est une situation désagréable, mais je crains que vous ne puissiez rien faire pour y remédier. Cessez de vous en plaindre et feignez d'aimer les petites bêtes. N'est-ce pas que les Français aiment les bêtes? Leur littérature en est chargée.
7. — Je saurais aimer un pigeon ou deux pigeons. Mais quand on en a des centaines et quand il faut en écouter les roucoulements depuis le matin jusqu'au soir, je ne m'attendris plus sur les oiseaux.
8. Je cherche de l'eau potable. Il doit y en avoir ici.
9. Quand on parlait des questions internationales, j'ai remarqué qu'il s'y intéressait énormément.
10. Quant aux directives de leurs syndicats, les ouvriers y obéissent rigoureusement.
11. Je ne suis pas étonné. Pourquoi le serais-je?
12. Ces avantages ne sont à la portée que des propriétaires qui disposent de capitaux importants.

13. Sa critique n'était pas toujours goûtée de ceux qui en étaient les victimes.
14. Un ami du défunt, très au courant de son œuvre, a complété le manuscrit inachevé en y adaptant des exemples simples, tirés des travaux cités en référence.
15. Le sel de cuisine ou chlorure de sodium, est un corps composé; l'électrolyse permet en effet d'en retirer deux corps nouveaux.
16. La femelle seule construit le nid, quoique son compagnon y participe aussi en y apportant des matériaux.
17. Je n'ai ni la prétention de traiter le problème à fond ni d'y apporter des conclusions nouvelles.
18. Paradoxalement on appelle "train de Paris" celui qui y va ou celui qui en vient.
19. Les réseaux ferroviaires qui, par suite de la cherté des traverses, sont obligés par tous les moyens, d'en prolonger la durée en service, évitent donc le système de la voie clouée pour y préférer celui de la voie vissée.
20. La connaissance des grandes formations géologiques du Canada est assez restreinte sauf auprès des géologues, des ingénieurs de mines ou des personnes directement intéressées à l'industrie minière.

C. In the following exercise read the French sentence and its translation given under *a*. Then rewrite the French sentence so that it will have the meaning indicated under *b*.

1. a. *Il fait partie de ce comité depuis quatre ans.*
   He has belonged to that committee for four years.
   b. He has belonged to it for four years.

2. a. *Pourquoi n'avez-vous pas répondu à sa lettre?*
   Why didn't you answer his letter?
   b. Why didn't you answer it?

3. a. *Il a beaucoup de livres.*
   He has a lot of books.
   b. He has a lot of them.

4. a. *Il n'est pas nécessaire d'insister sur sa stupidité.*
   It is not necessary to emphasize his stupidity.
   b. It is not necessary to emphasize it.

5. a. *Ce chapeau plaît à ma mère.*
   My mother likes this hat. (This hat pleases my mother.)
   b. She likes this hat.

LESSON X

Demonstrative Adjectives and Pronouns; Adverbs; Tout

[1]
DEMONSTRATIVE ADJECTIVES

THE forms of the demonstrative adjective are as follows:

MASC. SING.	FEM. SING.	PLURAL
ce *cet* } this, that	*cette* this, that	*ces* these, those

The meaning "this" or "that," "these" or "those" depends on the context. However, when the particles **-ci** and **là** are added to the noun, the meaning is restricted.

cet homme-ci et cette femme-là   this man and that woman

[2]
DEMONSTRATIVE PRONOUNS

Demonstrative pronouns are of two types: inflected and neuter.

	Inflected Form				Neuter Forms	
MASC. SING.	FEM. SING.	MASC. PLURAL	FEM. PLURAL			
celui	*celle*	*ceux*	*celles*	*ce*	*ceci*	*cela*

A] The inflected form has the following meanings:

celui-ci *celle-ci* } this one   *celui-là* *celle-là* } that one   *celui* *celle* } the one

ceux-ci *celles-ci* } these   *ceux-là* *celles-là* } those   *ceux* *celles* } the ones

Je vais utiliser un des magnéto-phones. Lequel est le meilleur, celui-ci ou celui qui est dans votre bureau?	I am going to use one of the tape-recorders. Which one is better, this one or the one which is in your office?
Jean m'a donné cette bague en or pour remplacer celle en argent que j'ai perdue.	John gave me this gold ring to re-place the silver one I lost.
Celui qui vous a dit cela a menti.	The one who told you that (who-ever told you that) lied.
Votre usine est plus moderne que celle de votre concurrent.	Your factory is more modern than your competitor's.

Note that the demonstrative pronouns are always followed by -ci, -là, by a relative pronoun, or by de (occasionally by some other preposition). When followed by de and a noun, as in the last example, the English equivalent is usually a noun in the possessive construction.

The most commonly forgotten point about *celui, celle, ceux*, and *celles* is that they can mean "the one" or "the ones."

The inflected form may have the following additional mean-ings:

celui-ci, celle-ci, ceux-ci, celles-ci	the latter
celui-là, celle-là, ceux-là, celles-là	the former

le physicien et le chimiste	celui-ci et celui-là
(*the physicist and the chemist*)	(*the latter and the former*)

Celui-ci means "the latter" in the sense of "this one" ("the nearer one," "the last-named one"). *Celui-là* means "the former" in the sense of "that one" ("the one farther away," "the one first men-tioned"). The forms with -ci are much more frequently used alone, as in the following examples:

Un regard jeté à la dérobée sur son patron suffit à le convaincre que celui-ci s'en tiendrait à sa résolu-tion.	A sidelong glance at his boss suf-ficed to convince him that the latter would stick to his resolu-tion (that he would stick to his resolution).
Puis quand on ajoute deux gouttes de ce liquide à un litre d'eau, celle-ci devient trouble.	Then when two drops of this liquid are added to a liter of water, the water becomes clouded.

Celle-ci refers to *eau*, the last feminine singular noun mentioned.

"The former" and "the latter" are awkward in many contexts in English and are much less frequent than *celui-ci, celle-ci, etc.*, in French. The French construction is a useful device for making a clear reference to one particular noun after various nouns of different gender and number have been used. In English it is often better to repeat the noun or, if the reference is clear, substitute "he," "she," "it," "they."

B] The neuter forms have the following meanings:
(1) *ceci:* this   *cela (ça)*[1]: that, it.

Qu'est-ce que c'est que cela?	What is that?
Dans sa dernière communication le professeur Dupont a dit ceci.	In his last report Professor Dupont made the following statement (had this to say).

Ceci and *cela* refer (1) to things that have not been previously mentioned, and for which, therefore, no gender or number has been established, and (2) to ideas.

Sometimes *cela* has no more than the value of "it."

(2) *Ce:* he, she, it, they, this, that, these, those.

Est-ce assez?	Is that (it) enough?
Sont-ce les chiffres que vous avez demandés?	Are they (those) the figures you asked for? (Is it the figures you asked for?)
C'est un bon médecin.	He is a good doctor.
C'est une bonne infirmière.	She is a good nurse.
Ce sont eux.	It is they.

Note that *ce sont* may be translated by "it is" (as well as "these are," "those are," "they are"). In English the verb "is" shows agreement with the preceding "it," whereas the French *sont* agrees with the plural noun or pronoun which follows.

The addition of the adverb *là* restricts the meaning of *ce* to "that" or "those" in the following sentences.

C'est *là* la meilleure solution.	*That* is the best solution.
Ce sont *là* des composés minéraux.	*Those* are mineral compounds.

---

[1] There is a strong tendency in French to use *là, voilà, cela* at the expense of their opposites *ici, voici, ceci*. So it is quite possible to find contexts in which *là* means "here," *voilà* means "here is," and *cela* means "this."

[3]
ADVERBS

A] The adverbial ending **-ment** is the equivalent of *-ly* in English and is usually added to the feminine singular of an adjective, but sometimes to other stems.

ADJECTIVE	ADVERB	
heureux, heureuse	heureusement	(*fortunately*)
net, nette	nettement	(*clearly*)
énorme	énormément	(*enormously*)

Note particularly the following words in which the stem is somewhat disguised.

ADJECTIVE	ADVERB	
courant	couramment	(*currently*)
nonchalant	nonchalamment	(*nonchalantly*)
récent	récemment	(*recently*)
prudent	prudemment	(*prudently*)

When the adjective ends in **-ant** or **-ent**, this ending is replaced by **-amment, -emment** in the corresponding adverb.[2]

B] The adverb *peu* deserves special attention because of its frequent use in a way that cannot be translated by "little" in English.

Ce composé chimique est peu stable.	This chemical compound is not very stable (is unstable).
Les enfants en sont peu contents.	The children are dissatisfied (not satisfied, not very well satisfied) with it.
Une telle issue est peu douteuse.	Such an outcome is almost certain.
Les ponts sont peu larges.	The bridges are narrow (not wide, not very wide).

Used before an adjective or adverb, *peu* is the equivalent of the English prefixes "in-," "un-," "non-," "not," "not very," or similar expressions.

Distinguish *peu* from *un peu*, "somewhat," used before an adjective or an adverb.

---

[2] They are actually pronounced the same, with [a] in the syllable preceding the **mm**.

Les rues sont un peu dangereuses la nuit.	The streets are somewhat dangerous at night.
Une telle issue est un peu douteuse.	Such an outcome is somewhat doubtful.

Peu de means "little," "few"; *un peu de* means "a little."

Ce sol contient peu d'azote.	This soil contains little nitrogen (does not contain much nitrogen).
Le sous-sol contient peu de minerais utilisables.	The substratum contains few ores that can be used.
Je voudrais un peu de sel.	I would like a little salt.

C] *Tout, bien, fort* are commonly used as adverbs synonymous with *très*.

$$\left. \begin{array}{l} \textit{bien poli} \\ \textit{fort poli} \\ \textit{tout poli} \end{array} \right\} \quad \text{very (quite) polite}$$

Il menait une vie bien tranquille.	He led a very peaceful life.
Vous le savez fort bien.	You know it very well.
Son appartement est tout petit.	His apartment is quite small.
Sa chambre est toute petite.	His room is quite small.

Note also the meaning of the adverbial *tout* in the following sentences:

Tout comme son père, il aimait la terre.	Just like his father, he loved the land.
Sa vie a été tout aussi triste que ses œuvres.	His life was just (quite) as sad as his works.

[4]
T O U T

This word appears in so many idiomatic expressions that it merits special study in the dictionary. Its original and most frequent usage is as an adjective and a pronoun. Note the following:

A] Singular adjective with indefinite article.

tout un réseau	a whole network
toute une bande	a whole band

B] Singular adjective with definite article.

tout le film	the whole film
toute la journée	the whole day, all day

C] Plural adjective, definite article.

tous les films	all the films, all films, every film
tous les hommes	all the men, all men, every man
tous les soirs	every evening
toutes les semaines	every week

D] Singular adjective without article.

tout être vivant	every (each, any) living being

E] Masculine singular pronoun *tout*, "everything."

tout ce qui	everything that, all that
tout ce que	everything (that), all (that)
tout ce qu'il y a de mieux	the very best there is

Je m'intéresse à tout ce qui concerne la philosophie.
: I take an interest in everything that concerns philosophy.

Il va obtenir tout ce que vous voulez.
: He is going to obtain everything you want (whatever you want).

C'est tout ce qu'il y a de frais et d'élégant.
: It is the very newest and most elegant. (It is the newest and most elegant imaginable.)

See *tout en* (Lesson III, paragraph 2).

[5]
IRREGULAR VERBS

Review the parts of the irregular verbs *courir*, *mourir*, *naître* in APPENDIX E.

[6]
IDIOMS

par cela même: by that very fact.

Additional idioms involving *tout*:
tout le monde: everyone.
tout de suite: immediately.
tout à coup: suddenly.

tout d'un coup: all of a sudden, suddenly.
tout au plus: at most.
tout au moins: at least.
tout d'abord: at first.

EXERCISES

A. Irregular verbs. Identify the tense and translate.

1. Je cours.
2. Je courais.
3. Je courrai.
4. Je courrais.
5. Ils courraient.
6. Ils couraient.
7. A-t-il couru?
8. Ils sont morts.
9. Ils étaient morts.
10. Elle mourut.
11. Nous mourons.
12. Nous mourrons.
13. Nous mourrions.
14. Naissant.
15. Il naît.[3]
16. Elle est née.
17. Elle était née.
18. Elle naquit.
19. Cela naissait.
20. Cela mourra.

[3] *Naître* is used much more often than "to be born" in English and is applied to a variety of things in the meaning "appear," "originate," and so on.

B. Adverbs. Write the masculine singular of the French adjective on which the adverb is formed. Translate the adverb.

1. fréquemment
2. différemment
3. intelligemment
4. décemment
5. récemment
6. brillamment
7. nonchalamment
8. patiemment
9. innocemment
10. prudemment
11. violemment
12. apparemment
13. indépendemment
14. ardemment
15. diligemment
16. élégamment
17. évidemment
18. méchamment
19. concurremment
20. couramment
21. vaillamment
22. bruyamment
23. puissamment
24. pesamment
25. savamment
26. consciemment
27. galamment
28. précédemment
29. complaisamment
30. étonnamment

Note: *Evidemment* usually has the meaning "obviously" or "of course" rather than "evidently."

C. Adverbs, continued. Translate.

1. peu poli
   peu patient
   peu instructif
   peu sûr
   peu fort

   peu instruit
   peu gentil
   peu adaptable
   peu nombreux
   peu ordinaire

   peu décent
   peu intelligent
   peu permanent
   peu clair
   peu souvent

2. un peu courant   un peu fréquent   un peu délicat
   peu courant   peu fréquent   peu délicat
   un peu dur
   peu dur

3. un peu plus pâle, un peu plus soucieux, un peu moins vite

4. trop peu décent, trop peu patient, assez peu adaptable, si peu imaginatif

5. un peu de lait   un peu d'enthousiasme   un peu de satisfaction
   peu de lait   peu d'enthousiasme   peu de satisfaction

6. peu de papier   peu d'argent   peu d'intérêt
   peu de stylos   peu de gens   peu d'hommes
   peu d'art moderne
   peu de meubles modernes

7. trop peu de soldats, trop peu de bons étudiants, fort peu de chose, trop
   peu de culture, fort peu d'amusements

8. bien grand, bien vite, tout petit, tout simplement, fort étrange

9. Mis à part le fait qu'il parle bien fort, il parle fort bien.

10. L'âge de ce manuscrit est assez peu sûr.

D. Idiomatic sentences. Translate.

1. C'était une scène triste. Tout n'était que ruine et confusion.
2. Le vieux musicien, en mourant, a laissé peu d'argent et peu d'amis.
3. Il me faut de nouveaux chapeaux; celui-ci n'est pas joli et celui que je portais hier n'est plus à la mode.
4. Ce sont les apparences qui vous trompent.
5. C'est là mon but.
6. Sont-ce les amis de votre père?
7. J'ai acheté une nouvelle maison juste à côté de celle d'Edouard.
8. On invita cinq médecins à examiner la malade. Ceux-ci, tout d'abord, ne se mirent pas d'accord sur le diagnostic.
9. Ses conseillers donnaient tous des avis intéressés.
10. Il avait un caractère violent tout comme son père. Mais celui-ci aurait su mieux se maîtriser à un moment critique.
11. La forme de l'éprouvette s'est peu modifiée depuis des siècles.
12. Pourquoi voulez-vous tout savoir?
13. Dernière née des machines parlantes, le magnétophone s'est révélé un incomparable instrument de critique et d'auto-critique.
14. On considère cet ouvrier comme irresponsable, mais ce n'est là qu'une partie de la vérité.
15. Tout en présentant de nombreuses analogies avec les danses d'autres pays, la danse coréenne a toutefois des particularités très marquées.
16. Afin d'obtenir des renseignements de plus en plus précis, les astronomes doivent porter une attention toute spéciale aux instruments utilisés.
17. Ce produit est un mélange intime d'une huile minérale et d'un savon de soude qui sert de support à l'huile; celle-ci est libérée par suite des températures ou des pressions.
18. Le rail doit s'appliquer étroitement sur la traverse ou sur une selle solidaire de celle-ci.

19. On n'arrivait à corriger le profil le long des rails qu'en introduisant des cales d'épaisseur variable entre ceux-ci et les traverses.

20. Aux passages à niveau les barrières ne s'ouvrent jamais assez vite au gré de l'automobiliste. Celui-ci manifeste alors son impatience à grands coups de klaxon.

E. Additional drill on the demonstrative pronoun. Translate.

1. ces fleurs et celles que vous m'avez jetées
2. ce volume et celui qui le précède
3. la maison en pierre et celle en briques
4. les tapis orientaux et tous ceux qui leur ressemblent
5. l'immeuble au coin et celui d'à côté
6. les lettres d'Anne et celles d'Antoine
7. le nouveau bureau de M. Lenard et celui, plus modeste, de son cousin
8. ces améliorations et celles qu'elles ont proposées

Relative Pronouns; Interrogative Pronouns; Impersonal Verbs

[1]
RELATIVE PRONOUNS

In English the relative pronoun "who" ("whom") is used for persons, "which" for things, and "that" for either one. In French, on the contrary, *qui* is used as the subject (persons or things), *que* as the object (persons or things), and a distinction is made between persons and things only with the object of a preposition: *qui* (or *lequel*) for persons and *lequel* for things.

	PERSONS		THINGS	
SUBJECT	*qui*	who, that	*qui*	which, that
OBJECT	*que*	whom, that	*que*	which, that
OBJECT OF PREPOSITION	*qui* *lequel*	}whom, that	*lequel*	which, that

où   where, when, in which, at which

dont   whose, of whom/which, from whom/which

Note: *Lequel* has four forms: *lequel, laquelle, lesquels, lesquelles.* Contractions occur with *à* and *de: auquel, duquel, desquels,* etc.

A] The fact that *que* can never be the subject of a verb must be constantly borne in mind because it often occurs in the normal position of the subject. The French are fond of inverted relative clauses: *que* + verb + subject. If *que* (*qu'*) is immediately followed by a verb, look beyond the verb for the subject.[1]

Les animaux que pourront voir les enfants...	The animals that the children will be able to see . . .

[1] Those who know Spanish must be careful to avoid any subconscious carryover from that language, where *que* can be both subject and object.

| Les théories qu'a soutenues le géologue... | The theories that the geologist has supported . . . |
| Le seul défaut de la pièce est le rôle exagéré qu'y joue le roi. | The only defect in the play is the exaggerated role that the king plays in it. |

Qu' is equivalent to *que*, never *qui*.[2] The following sentences illustrate how important it is to interpret correctly the use of the relative pronoun.

| Le voleur qui a blessé l'agent de police... | The thief that wounded the policeman . . . |
| Le voleur qu'a blessé l'agent de police... | The thief that the policeman wounded . . . |

The order of the items in the French inverted relative clause can be retained in English by changing the verb to the passive voice in translation. This is particularly desirable when the subject is long.

| Le voleur qu'a blessé l'agent de police... | The thief that was wounded by the policeman . . . |
| Ce poème offre des scènes variées qu'unit pourtant un thème central. | This poem offers varied scenes, which are nevertheless unified by a central theme. |

B] *Dont* represents *de* + a relative pronoun (*de qui, duquel, de laquelle, desquels, desquelles*). *Où* represents *à, sur, dans* (but not *de*) and a relative pronoun.

(1) *Dont* can include all the meanings that *de* can have; it can be translated "whose," "of whom/which," "from whom/which," etc., and even "which" or "whom" when its use is required in an idiom containing a *de*.

Les choses *dont* il parle ne vous regardent pas.	The things (*that*) he talks *about* (The things *about which* he talks) do not concern you.
M. Beaulieu est le professeur *dont* j'ai suivi le cours l'année dernière.	Mr. Beaulieu is the professor *whose* course I took last year.
Je n'aime pas la façon *dont* il vous parle. (*de cette façon* in this way)	I do not like the way (*in which*) he speaks to you.
Les choses *dont* je me souviens... (*se souvenir de* remember)	The things (*that*) I remember . . .

[2] The only French word in which the *i* is elided before a vowel is *si*, and then only in the combinations *s'il* and *s'ils*.

It can be seen from these examples and others that in English the relative pronoun is often merely understood, whereas in French it is always expressed.

(2) Observe the use of *dont* meaning "whose."

Est-ce M. Beaulieu *dont le fils* est votre médecin?	Is it Mr. Beaulieu *whose son* is your doctor?
Est-ce M. Beaulieu *dont* vous avez suivi *le cours?*	Is it Mr. Beaulieu *whose course* you took?

In English "whose" always precedes the reference to the person or thing possessed, whereas *dont* is separated from it if it is the object of the verb, as in the second example. In this case French has the customary word order (subject + verb + object), and English the inversion. Another difference: the noun following *dont* always has an article; in English the noun following "whose" does not.

(3) *Où*, being the equivalent of *auquel, dans lequel*, and so on, can have all the meanings of these prepositional phrases and can also be translated "where" or "when." *Où* means "when" after nouns of time (*jour, moment, époque*).

Voilà la maison *où* je suis né.	There is the house *where* (*in which*) I was born.
L'époque *où* régnait François I était brillante.	The period *when* Francis I reigned was brilliant.

(4) The function of *dont* and *où* as relative pronouns is similar to that of *en* and *y* as personal pronouns.

La France a besoin *de ces matières premières.*	France needs *those raw materials.*
La France *en* a besoin.	France needs *them.*
Nous parlons des matières premières *dont* la France a besoin.	We are talking about the raw materials (*which*) France needs.
Marie habite *dans la nouvelle maison.*	Mary lives *in the new house.*
Marie *y* habite.	Mary lives *there* (*in it*).
Nous connaissons la nouvelle maison *où* (*dans laquelle*) Marie habite.	We know the new house *where* Mary lives (*that* Mary lives *in*).

C] The compound relative pronouns *ce qui, ce que* mean "what" ("that which"), "which," "the fact that."

Je savais ce qu'il voulait dire.	I knew what he meant.
Il a signalé ce que fait la France à cet égard.	He pointed out what France is doing in this respect.
La balance reprend sa position d'équilibre, ce qui indique qu'il n'y a eu aucune variation de masse.	The scale resumes its position of balance, which indicates that there has been no variation in mass (or, the scale resumes its position of balance; this indicates . . .).
Il a demandé un emprunt de cent mille francs. Ce qui, comme je vous le disais, est absurde.	He asked for a loan of 100,000 francs. This, as I was saying, is ridiculous.
Cela tient à ce que le Français boit peu de lait.	That is due to the fact that the Frenchman drinks little milk.

When *ce qui, ce que* refer to a whole clause (third and fourth examples), they are translated "which." In this usage they are preceded by a comma, sometimes by a period. "Which" referring to a whole clause is not considered choice usage in English: if "this" or "that" is substituted, the punctuation must, of course, change.

Ce que (*ce qu'*) may also be followed by inverted word order as in the case of simple *que* (*qu'*). Note the second of the five examples above.

[2]
INTERROGATIVE PRONOUNS

A] The invariable forms of the interrogative pronouns are as follows:

	PERSONS		THINGS	
SUBJECT	*qui* *qui est-ce qui* }	who?	*qu'est-ce qui*	what?
OBJECT	*qui* *qui est-ce que* }	whom?	*que* *qu'est-ce que* }	what?
OBJECT OF PREPOSITION	*qui* whom?		*quoi* what?	

The three alternate long forms are sometimes seen, especially *qu'est-ce que*, and are usually easily understood. They are given here chiefly to be contrasted with the one required long form, *qu'est-ce qui*, "what," which *is* often misinterpreted.

| Qu'est-ce qui vous fait rire ? | What is making you laugh ? |
| Qu'est-ce qui rend la terre si verte ? | What makes the earth so green ? |

B] Note the following idiomatic use of *qu'est-ce que* (*qu'est-ce que c'est que*) to inquire into the nature of something, to ask for a definition. When the question becomes indirect (second example following), the formula is *ce qu'est* (*ce que c'est que*).

| Qu'est-ce que la psychologie ex-périmentale ? | What is experimental psychology ? |
| Je vais vous dire ce qu'est (ce que c'est que) la psychologie expéri-mentale. | I will tell you what experimental psychology is. |

C] The variable interrogative pronoun *lequel, laquelle, lesquels, lesquelles* means "which one?" "which ones?"

[3]
IMPERSONAL VERBS

Some French verbs are always used impersonally; for example, *il faut, il pleut* (like English "it is raining"). Others, however, which usually have a personal subject, may be introduced by the impersonal *il* with the real subject following the verb (compare the English "a time came when . . ." and "there came a time when . . ."). Usually the subject has to be put back in its normal position in translation.

Je surveillais Jean pendant qu'il faisait ses devoirs.	I was keeping an eye on John while he did his homework.
Il faisait froid. (*impers.*)	It was cold.
Le vieux monsieur n'avait pas de voiture. Il est arrivé un peu tard.	The old gentleman had no car. He arrived somewhat late.
Il est arrivé des colis pour vous. (*impers.*)	Some parcels have arrived for you.
Quand on fait agir l'acide chlor-hydrique sur du zinc, il se forme du chlorure de zinc.	When you cause hydrochloric acid to act on zinc, zinc chloride is formed.

[4]
IRREGULAR VERBS

Review the forms of the irregular verbs *conduire, suivre, envoyer, recevoir* in APPENDIX E.

[5]
IDIOMS

il est: there is, there are (= *il y a*).
il en est de même: the same thing is true.
il en résulte: the result is, the consequence is.
c'est que: it is because, the reason is that.

La vie ici leur semble très difficile. C'est qu'ils ne se sont pas faits à notre climat.	Life seems very difficult to them here. It is because they have not become accustomed to our climate.

de quoi: enough, the wherewithal.

Il a de quoi vivre.	He has enough to live on.

à quoi bon (+ inf.)?: what's the use of?

A quoi bon s'en plaindre?	What's the use of complaining about it?

envoyer chercher: to send for (= *faire venir*).

EXERCISES

A. Irregular verbs. Identify the tense and translate.

1. Il conduit.
2. N'enverras-tu pas?
3. Je suis.
4. Je suivais.
5. Il ne recevrait pas.
6. Ils reçurent.
7. Conduisit-il?
8. Bien qu'il conduise.
9. Reçoivent-ils?
10. Elles envoyèrent.
11. Nous ne conduisions pas.
12. Quoiqu'il conduisît.
13. Recevez.
14. N'envoyons pas.
15. N'envoyons-nous pas?
16. Ils se sont suivis.
17. Ont-ils reçu?
18. Se sont-ils reçus?
19. Ils ne s'étaient pas suivis.
20. Ils enverront.

B. Translate.

1. Je leur faisais remarquer le soin qu'avait pris le scribe en transcrivant ce manuscrit.
2. Nous savons tous l'influence qu'a eue ce projet européen.
3. Savez-vous ce qu'est devenu le héros de cette aventure?
4. Le guide m'a montré ce qu'il considérait comme étant les endroits les plus historiques.
5. Ces données ne sont pas tout à fait identiques aux faits que raconte sa biographie.
6. Qu'est-ce qui supporte le toit de la maison?
7. Qu'est-ce qui est arrivé?

8. Qui est arrivé?
9. J'ai remarqué la belle serviette dont le plat était recouvert.
10. Il se sert de ce dictionnaire.
   Il s'en sert.
   Voici le dictionnaire dont il se sert.
11. M. Dufour s'est plaint du bruit. Sa femme s'en est plainte aussi.
12. Qu'est-ce qui vous a donné envie de lire ce roman-là?
13. Puis il s'est passé une chose très curieuse.
14. Qu'est-ce que vous avez donné comme pourboire?
15. Il parlait d'une façon affectée. Tout le monde a remarqué la façon dont il parlait.
16. Nous faisons partie du cercle français. Est-ce que vous en faites partie? Dressez-moi une liste de toutes les organisations dont vous faites partie.
17. Ce qui m'intéresse à ce sujet, ce sont les travaux pratiques au cours desquels les étudiants complètent leur instruction théorique.
18. Voilà un fait dont enfin il se rend compte.
19. Marcel est l'ami dont vous avez vu la photographie dans mon appartement.
20. Il m'a regardé d'un sourire bienveillant, comme si ce que j'allais dire n'avait surement aucune importance.
21. Je peux me tenir au courant par la lecture d'un journal parisien que me prête assez régulièrement mon voisin.
22. Je suis toujours émerveillé de voir l'espèce d'admiration que leur inspire cet homme, pourtant si simple d'aspect.
23. Le renseignement que nous donne la lumière sur la position de l'électron n'est pas valable, puisque l'électron n'est plus à l'endroit où l'a trouvé la lumière, lorsque celle-ci vient nous communiquer son information.
24. Il ne viendrait à personne l'idée de traverser l'Atlantique à la nage.
25. Dans cette revue on trouve des études sur les problèmes qu'ont à résoudre les gouvernements, ainsi que des articles sur l'actualité internationale.
26. Nous allons étudier les substances élémentaires que fournit la terre à l'homme.
27. Il manquait à ses recherches un ensemble expérimental cohérent, permettant de mener ses découvertes à leur terme.
28. On constate que les revues scientifiques publient toujours davantage d'articles sur la séismologie. C'est que celle-ci constitue le moyen d'investigation le plus puissant dont on dispose actuellement pour l'étude de l'intérieur du globe.
29. Il est une autre façon d'apprécier le perfectionnement des techniques, c'est d'en constater les effets sur le plan économique et social, surtout en ce qui concerne le prix demandé à l'usager.
30. La lexicologie conduit vers les bases philosophiques d'une langue: Qu'est-ce qu'un mot? Qu'est-ce que son contenu conceptuel?

C. Read the following sentences and write out the French equivalent of the English in parentheses.

1. Vous connaissez les fatigues (*which*) comporte un voyage.
2. Voilà (*what*) m'occupe.
3. Faites (*what*) vous a dit madame.
4. (*What*) vous a fait crier?
5. J'ai acheté ces melons un franc pièce, (*which*) m'a économisé trois francs.

LESSON XII

Special Uses of the Future and Conditional Tenses; Conditional Sentences

[1]
SPECIAL USES OF THE FUTURE AND CONDITIONAL TENSES

A] In the following sentences French employs the future or future perfect, whereas English uses the present or present perfect.

Je vous serai reconnaissant tant que je *vivrai*.

I will be grateful to you as long as I *live*.

Aussitôt qu'il *aura trouvé* votre porte-monnaie, il vous le renverra.

As soon as he *has found* your billfold, he will send it back to you.

A principle of French grammar is that if the main clause is in the future tense the subordinate clause is also stated in the future or future perfect tense after conjunctions of time (not, however, after *si*).

B] The future and conditional tenses and their compound forms are often used to express probability or possibility.

Je ne les vois pas. Ils seront déjà partis.

I do not see them. They must have already left (have probably already left).

Il ne m'a pas écrit depuis longtemps. Serait-il vexé?

He has not written to me for a long time. Could he be angry? (Is it possible that he is angry?)

Est-ce que vous auriez pu vous tromper en recueillant ces données?

Could you have made a mistake in gathering these data? (Is it possible that you made a mistake in gathering these data?)

C] Another usage, closely allied with the preceding, is the employment of the conditional perfect instead of the past tense (or conditional instead of present) to show that the writer denies responsibility for the statement.

L'accusé aurait avoué le vol en parlant à l'aubergiste.	The accused man supposedly admitted the theft while talking to the innkeeper.
Selon ce livre, Napoléon lui-même n'aurait eu aucune confiance dans la traction à vapeur.	According to this book, Napoleon himself had no confidence in steam traction.

In English this denial is achieved either by the use of an adverb such as "supposedly," "allegedly," or "presumably" or by the mention of the source ("according to this new book").

[2]
CONDITIONAL SENTENCES

A] In its simplest form the French conditional sentence has a tense sequence similar to that of English.

Si je reçois son rapport, je vous l'enverrai.	If I receive his report, I will send it to you.
Si Jean reste, moi je m'en vais.	If John stays, I go.

If there is more than one "if" clause, the second is introduced by *que* and is in the subjunctive.[1]

Si ce petit pendule est suspendu et qu'on le fasse osciller, on pourra constater tout ce que je viens de décrire.	If this little pendulum is suspended and (if it) is made to oscillate, you will be able to observe everything that I have just described.

B] A certain common type of sentence, called the "contrary-to-fact conditional," in its simplest form involves the following tense sequence.

S'il voyait cela, il serait furieux.	If he saw that, he would be furious.
S'il avait vu cela, il aurait été furieux.	If he had seen that, he would have been furious.

The "if" clause takes the imperfect or pluperfect tense; the conclusion takes the conditional or conditional perfect tense.

---

[1] It is characteristic of French that the conjunction is not repeated but is replaced by *que* on a second or third round: *parce que ... et que...*; *lorsque ... et que...*, etc.

Observe that the imperfect tense used in this conditional sentence lacks the three possible meanings mentioned in Lesson II, paragraph 2, for the imperfect. The English equivalent here is simply "If he saw."

C] Several variations on the preceding pattern may be encountered, particularly in literary style. "Even if," "even though" is expressed by *quand* or *quand même* followed by the conditional or conditional perfect. In this case the conditional (or conditional perfect) tense is found in both clauses.

Quand bien (même) il verrait cela, il serait indifférent.	Even if he saw that, he would be indifferent.
Quand (même) il aurait vu cela, il aurait été indifférent.	Even if he had seen that, he would have been indifferent.

D] Another variation, common in literary style, is the use of the pluperfect subjunctive in either or both parts of the conditional sentence.

Si ce phénomène se fût produit, il eût été reconnu.	If this phenomenon had occurred, it would have been recognized.
Une telle action lui eût valu un prix.	Such an action would have won him a prize.

As in the second example, the condition may be merely implied. *Eût* and *fût* are the subjunctive forms most frequently used with a conditional meaning. When these words are found in a main clause (the subjunctive is normally used in a subordinate clause), they can be considered the equivalents of *aurait* and *serait*.

E] For the foreigner the most elusive form of the French conditional contrary-to-fact sentence is the following.

Il passerait toute sa vie à écrire, qu'il ne produirait rien d'intéressant.	If he spent his whole life writing, he would not produce anything interesting.

When both clauses are in the conditional tense and are connected by *que*, the first one is the "if" clause.

F] If *si* is followed by the imperfect tense, but by no other clause, it means "what if," "what about," "suppose."

Si Charles nous surprenait!	What if Charles surprised us?
Si on inventait un nouveau style d'architecture!	Suppose we invent a new style of architecture!

G] In French, as in English, it is possible to show the conditional clause merely by inversion. (*Were he to see me, he would recognize me immediately. Should I find one, I'll buy it.*) When this inversion takes place in French, the verb is often thrown into the subjunctive.

Il allait gagner une fortune, dût-il recourir aux moyens les plus brutaux.	He was going to win a fortune if he had to resort to the most brutal means.

(Note that *dût-il = s'il dût = s'il devait.*)

H] *Si* and *quand même* have other meanings besides those mentioned for conditional sentences. Note the following:

Si may introduce an indirect question in the meaning "whether" or "if" and may then be followed by any tense.

Il sait toujours si l'expérience a réussi.	He always knows whether the experiment has succeeded.

Quand même as an adverb means "nevertheless," "all the same."

Il le fera quand même.	He will do it just the same.

[3]
IRREGULAR VERBS

Review the forms of *prendre, suffire, rire* in APPENDIX E.

[4]
IDIOMS

il suffit de   (it) is sufficient, enough

Il suffit d'un regard pour vous montrer de quoi il s'agit.	A glance is sufficient to show you what it is about.
Il suffit d'appeler si l'on désire du service.	It is sufficient to call if you wish service.

Il suffit de may be followed by a noun or an infinitive; if a noun follows, as in the first example, this noun must become the subject of the English verb in translation.

la partie   part; game, match

faire partie de: to belong to, to be a member of.

le parti   (political) party; decision

prendre un parti: to reach a decision.
prendre le parti de (+inf.): to decide (to do something).
prendre le parti de (*quelqu'un*): to take someone's side.

la part   portion, share, part

faire part d'une chose à quelqu'un: to inform someone about a thing.

(Observe also the use of *la part* in the various adverbial expressions: *quelque part; nulle part; d'une part ... d'autre part; de part et d'autre; à part.*)

EXERCISES

A. Irregular verbs. Identify the tense and translate.

1. Il prend.	11. N'auriez-vous pas pris?
2. Il prit.	12. Il part.
3. Prîmes-nous?	13. Elle est partie.
4. Il aurait pris.	14. N'étaient-ils pas partis?
5. Cela suffit-il?	15. Ils rient.
6. Cela ne suffisait pas.	16. Ils rirent.
7. Prenons.	17. Nous riions.
8. Ils prirent.	18. Bien que nous ne riions pas.
9. Il faut qu'il prenne.	19. Bien qu'il soit parti.
10. Ils ne prendraient pas.	20. Il surprendrait.

B. Translate.

1. Qu'est-ce que votre professeur dirait s'il vous entendait exprimer de tels sentiments?
2. Qu'aurait-il dit s'il vous avait entendu parler ainsi?
3. Quand bien même vous le lui expliqueriez, il ne vous croirait pas.
4. Vous le lui expliqueriez dix fois, qu'il ne vous comprendrait pas.
5. Si vous le lui expliquiez!
6. Demandez-lui s'il a étudié la mécanique appliquée.
7. On eût recommencé le travail tout de suite si nous y avions consenti.
8. Un ingénieur français aurait effectué un vol de quelques mètres dix ans avant les frères Wright.
9. S'il m'avait dit de m'asseoir, je me serais assis.
10. Les deux jeunes filles n'auraient pas été plus surprises si un fantôme était apparu devant elles.
11. Ce petit livre n'était que l'abrégé d'un document plus ample que l'auteur aurait eu à sa disposition.

12. Il est impossible de traduire sa prose en anglais et quand même ce serait possible, la génération moderne n'apprécierait pas ses sentiments.
13. Il suffit d'un mot pour le rassurer.
14. Ils prirent le parti de résister de toutes leurs forces.
15. Les Etats-Unis font partie des Nations-Unies.
16. A quoi bon hésiter si longtemps? Il faut prendre un parti.
17. L'écriteau n'est plus à sa place. Il aura sans doute été emporté par le vent.
18. Si Jean se marie avant la fin de l'année et que sa famille approuve le choix de son épouse, il doit hériter d'une somme considérable.
19. Le copiste de ce vieux manuscrit eût dû être d'une négligence assez peu ordinaire pour faire tant de fautes; donc il s'agit de fautes commises par l'auteur.
20. Quand même chaque édition aurait un index, il serait pourtant commode d'avoir à sa disposition une table générale, formant en quelque sorte le résumé de tous les index particuliers.
21. L'auteur de la grammaire a parfaitement raison en laissant aux maîtres le plaisir de fournir à leurs élèves tous les renseignements historiques qui leur paraîtront utiles.
22. Si un corps existait dans le vide, ce serait un non-sens de dire qu'il est en repos ou en mouvement.
23. On a provisoirement divisé les roches de la surface de la lune en trois formations d'âge pré-marin, marin et post-marin. Les plus vieilles, ou roches d'âge pré-marin, auraient été désagrégées au cours des âges par des milliers d'explosions survenues lors de la chute de météorites.
24. Fréquemment on impute au savant le chômage que créerait l'automation; on devrait plutôt le louer d'avoir fait progresser la médecine et d'avoir amélioré l'alimentation.
25. Pris entre ses obligations de service public, d'une part, et la nécessité de défendre son trafic contre ses concurrents, le chemin de fer ne voyait s'ouvrir devant lui qu'une seule issue: un meilleur rendement.

C. Translate the following sentence into English; then perform the operations indicated.

S'il vendait sa bicyclette, il retournerait chez lui à pied.

1. Rewrite the French sentence so that it would mean: If he had sold his bicycle, he would have returned home on foot.
2. Rewrite the sentence so that it would mean: Even if he sold his bicycle, he would not return home on foot. [TWO WAYS: (a) starting with *quand même*, (b) using *que*, as in paragraph 2e of this lesson.]
3. Rewrite to mean: Even if he had sold his bicycle, he would not have returned home on foot. [TWO WAYS: (a) *quand même*, (b) *que*.]
4. Translate into French. What if he sold his bicycle!

LESSON XIII

The Subjunctive

ABILITY to recognize all verb forms immediately is indispensable to accurate reading of French. Among the forms that must be known are the four tenses of the subjunctive which occur in the written language.

The subjunctive shows an action or condition as demanded or desired, etc. English, too, has the subjunctive, although it is much less common than in French. It can be seen in sentences such as the following: (1) I suggest that the matter *be dropped*. (Indicative expression of the idea: "The matter is dropped." "The matter is being dropped." "The matter will be dropped.") (2) I wish my father *were* rich. (Indicative: "My father is rich.")

[1]
REVIEW OF THE FORMS OF THE SUBJUNCTIVE

Review in the Tables of Verb Forms in APPENDIX E the subjunctive of the three regular conjugations and of the irregular verbs *avoir* and *être*.

This review can be simplified by the following observations.

A] The endings of the PRESENT SUBJUNCTIVE are the same for all verbs except *avoir* and *être*.

REGULAR PRES. SUBJ. ENDINGS		*AVOIR*	*ETRE*
je donne	je voie	j'aie	je sois
tu donnes	tu voies	tu aies	tu sois
il donne	il voie	il ait	il soit
nous donnions	nous voyions	nous ayons	nous soyons
vous donniez	vous voyiez	vous ayez	vous soyez
ils donnent	ils voient	ils aient	ils soient

The stem of the present subjunctive is described in the introduction to APPENDIX E as being the present participial stem of regular verbs. An even broader statement, which would include most irregular verbs, is to say that the stem of the present subjunctive is usually the same as that of the third person plural of the present indicative: ils **donn**ent, ils **finiss**ent, ils **vend**ent, ils **voi**ent, ils **connaiss**ent, and so on.

Certain present subjunctive stems are irregular and must be memorized: *j'aille* (*aller*), *je fasse* (*faire*), *je sache* (*savoir*), *je puisse* (*pouvoir*), *je veuille* (*vouloir*), *je vaille* (*valoir*).

Some irregular verbs have two different stems in the present subjunctive, reflecting two stems in the present indicative. Most common are *aller, boire, devoir, recevoir, venir, tenir, prendre, mourir, vouloir, valoir*. As an example, observe the double stem of *devoir*.

PRES. IND.	PRES. SUBJ.
je dois	je doive
tu dois	tu doives
il doit	il doive
nous devons	nous devions
vous devez	vous deviez
ils doivent	ils doivent

B] The endings of the IMPERFECT SUBJUNCTIVE are the same for all verbs: **-sse, -sses, -ˆt, -ssions, -ssiez, -ssent.**

je donnasse	je vendisse	je lusse	je vinsse
tu donnasses	tu vendisses	tu lusses	tu vinsses
il donnât	il vendît	il lût	il vînt
nous donnassions	nous vendissions	nous lussions	nous vinssions
vous donnassiez	vous vendissiez	vous lussiez	vous vinssiez
ils donnassent	ils vendissent	ils lussent	ils vinssent

The *stem* of the imperfect subjunctive is identical with that of the past definite indicative minus the last letter: donnaí, vendiś, luś, allaí, euś, fuś, vinś. The stem always ends in **a, i, u,** or **in** (*in* only in the past definite stems of *venir, tenir,* and their compounds).

C] The TWO COMPOUND TENSES OF THE SUBJUNCTIVE are formed according to the pattern of the indicative, that is, the subjunctive of the auxiliary verb and the past participle.

[2]
OVERLAPPING SUBJUNCTIVE AND INDICATIVE FORMS

A] In first-conjugation verbs the present subjunctive is identical with the present indicative in four forms: all forms of the singular and the third person plural (see Verb Tables in APPENDIX E).

B] In second-conjugation verbs the present and imperfect subjunctives are identical except for the third person singular (see the present and imperfect subjunctive of *finir* in APPENDIX E).

C] In the vast majority of French verbs the first and second person plural of the present subjunctive are identical with the first and second person plural of the imperfect indicative.

[3]
MEANINGS OF THE SUBJUNCTIVE IN SUBORDINATE CLAUSES

A] The subjunctive, as its name implies, is to be found chiefly in subordinate clauses: after main clauses containing verbs of volition, emotion, doubt, negation; after most impersonal expressions in the main clauses; after certain conjunctions.

B] For a reading knowledge there is no necessity to review all of these uses; the meaning of a French subjunctive is often the same as that of the corresponding indicative tense or the context easily suggests the English equivalent. Note the following examples:

PRESENT SUBJUNCTIVE

Il est possible qu'il vienne tout seul. — It is possible that he is coming (comes, does come, may come, will come) all alone.

PRESENT PERFECT SUBJUNCTIVE

Il est possible qu'il soit venu tout seul. — It is possible that he came (has come) all alone.

IMPERFECT SUBJUNCTIVE

Il était possible qu'il vînt tout seul. — It was possible that he would come (was coming, might come) all alone.

PLUPERFECT SUBJUNCTIVE

Il était possible qu'il fût venu tout seul. — It was possible that he had come all alone.

These examples illustrate the usual span of meanings of each of the four subjunctive tenses and its relationship to the tense of the main clause. Particularly to be avoided is the notion, fostered by the verb paradigms of many textbooks, that the subjunctive must necessarily mean "may" or "might."

C] Although the meanings of the subjunctive in subordinate clauses are usually quite like the indicative, there are some cases in which idioms of French and English are at variance.

(1) The French present subjunctive is often used where English would use a future indicative. Compare the first example in paragraph B with the following:

J'ai peur que ses questions ne mettent votre patience à l'épreuve.	I am afraid his questions will try your patience.
Il se donne énormément de peine pour que son expérience réussisse.	He is going to an enormous amount of trouble so that his experiment will succeed.

(2) French takes a subjunctive clause after *vouloir*; English employs an infinitive construction after "want."

Voulez-vous qu'il s'en aille?	Do you want him to go away?
Il veut que je parle.	He wants me to speak.

Note the difference in meaning of the next two sentences.

Il veut que je parle.	He wants me to speak.
Il veut me parler.	He wants to speak to me.

In the second sentence *il* is the subject of both *veut* and *parler*, and *me* is the object of *parler*.

(3) The conjunction *sans que* is followed by a clause in the subjunctive. In English "without" is a preposition. Therefore, in expressing this kind of construction in English, the French subjunctive verb must be translated as a gerund. *Sans que* may also mean "unless."

Partez sans qu'ils le sachent.	Leave without their knowing it.

(4) *Pour que*, "in order that," "so that," is a conjunction followed by the subjunctive. It sometimes has the meaning illustrated in the following:

Pour que le point soit en mouvement, il suffit évidemment qu' une seule de ses coordonnées dépende de t.	For the point to be in movement it obviously suffices that only one of its coordinates depend on t.

(The *que* is never a relative pronoun after *pour*; the ideas "for whom" and "for which" are expressed in French by *pour qui, pour lequel*, etc. See Lesson XI, paragraph 1, Object of Preposition.)

(5) *Qui, quoi, quelque, pour*, etc., followed by a subjunctive clause express the ideas of "whoever," "whatever," "however" in a concessive sense.

(a) Whoever.

Qui que vous soyez, vous avez bien trompé tout le monde.	Whoever you may be, you have certainly fooled everyone.

(b) Whatever (as a pronoun, and as an adjective).

Quoi que ce soit, il en a été très ennuyé.	Whatever it is, he has been quite annoyed by it.
Quel que soit son mouvement, les distances mutuelles des points d'un corps solide restent invariables.	Whatever its movement may be, the mutual distances of the points of a solid body remain invariable.
Quelques fautes que l'auteur ait commises, nous le lisons avec plaisir.	Whatever mistakes the author may have made, we read him with pleasure.

(c) However.

Quelque brave qu'il soit... (Aussi) si brave qu'il soit... Pour brave qu'il soit... Tout brave qu'il soit (est)...	However brave he may be ... (no matter how brave he is ...)
Si faibles que soient les courants électriques...	However weak the electric currents may be ...

The pattern for these concessive "however" clauses is

$$\left.\begin{array}{l} \textit{pour} \\ \textit{si} \\ \textit{quelque} \\ \textit{tout} \end{array}\right\} + \text{adjective (or adverb)} + \text{subjunctive clause,}$$

but *tout* may also be followed by the indicative.

(6) *Que ... ou (que)*... followed by verbs in the subjunctive means "whether . . . or . . ." A variant of this is *soit que...ou que....*

Qu'il s'agisse d'une seule personne ou de plusieurs, on applique les mêmes règles.	Whether it is a question of one person or of several, the same rules are applied.

The many uses of *que* make this one easy to overlook. It is indicated not only by the occurrence of the subjunctive but also by the punctuation, for it is always set off by commas.

[4]
THE USE OF THE SUBJUNCTIVE IN MAIN CLAUSES

A] The present subjunctive may appear in the main clause, usually introduced by *que,* to express a formal wish. A similar wish in English would begin with "let" or "may."

Qu'il entre.	Let him come in.
Maintenant, que le gagnant se montre magnanime.	Now let the winner show himself magnanimous.

B] The imperfect subjunctive and the pluperfect subjunctive are used in the main clause to replace the conditional and the conditional perfect. The pluperfect subjunctive is more common in this usage (see Lesson XII, paragraph 2d).

[5]
IRREGULAR VERBS

Review the irregular verbs *croire, croître, plaire, pleuvoir* in Appendix E.

[6]
IDIOMS

Que (Comme)... (adjective or adverb)!:　How...!

Qu'il est bon!	How kind he is!
Que ce problème est compliqué!	How complicated that problem is!
Comme elle peint bien!	How well she paints!

Que de (Combien de):   How many! So many! What a lot of!

Avez-vous visité une des nouvelles usines hydroélectriques? Que de progrès depuis la première installation!	Have you visited one of the new hydroelectric plants? What a lot of progress since the first installation!

soit: or

soit . . . soit: either . . . or (= *ou . . . ou*)

soit que . . . soit que: whether . . . or (whether)

Soit as a conjunction is to be carefully distinguished from *soit* as the subjunctive of *être*.

EXERCISES

A. Irregular verbs. Identify the tense and translate.

1. Il croit.	6. N'a-t-il pas plu?
2. Ils crurent.	7. Ça ne plairait pas.
3. Croissant.	8. Avait-il crû?
4. Il pleuvrait.	9. Aurais-tu plu?
5. Elle plaisait.	10. Il ne pleuvait pas.

B. Identification of subjunctive forms. The following verbs are all in the subjunctive. Name the infinitive of each one. (Do not translate.)

1. il plaigne	14. ils lussent
2. ils aillent	15. ils tinssent
3. nous portions	16. nous puissions
4. vous fussiez	17. ils prennent
5. vous sachiez	18. il connaisse
6. ils vaillent	19. il voie
7. je fasse	20. il vît
8. il fît	21. ils reçussent
9. il doive	22. nous pussions
10. il boive	23. ils finissent
11. ils soient	24. ils croient
12. tu aies	25. ils croissent
13. il veuille	

C. Translate.

1. Est-ce que votre père veut que vous vous fassiez mathématicien?
2. Pour courageux qu'il soit, il n'en craint pas moins la mort.
3. Il est peu vraisemblable que nous nous soyons connus avant.
4. De quelque région qu'ils soient, les Français aiment Paris.

5. Pourquoi défendez-vous que nous étudiions ensemble?
6. Il veut nous dire quelque chose.
7. Si vaillants que soient ses adversaires, c'est lui qui l'emportera.
8. Cette tâche est trop difficile pour que nous puissions l'accomplir.
9. Quoiqu'elle fût guérie, elle ne voulut pas le croire.
10. Nous avons craint qu'elle ne perdît patience et s'en allât sans nous avertir.
11. Quelques propos qu'on ait tenus au sujet de sa démission, ce que je vous dis est la vérité.
12. Est-il possible qu'il se soit blessé?
13. Le monde s'en fût scandalisé s'il l'eût su.
14. Que je suis content de vous revoir!
15. Nous avons achevé notre travail dehors. Qu'il pleuve maintenant!
16. Au mois de juin j'ai parcouru toute la ferme. Que de belles fleurs! Que de beaux arbres!
17. Que le petit garçon est sage!
18. Que le petit garçon soit sage!
19. L'arbuste croissait rapidement sans qu'on s'en aperçût.
20. Il est possible qu'il croisse plus rapidement encore.
21. Je saurai te retrouver où que tu te caches.
22. Certes, cet homme n'eût dû leur inspirer que pitié.
23. Si hauts que la naissance ou la richesse nous ait placés, on a toujours ses responsabilités.
24. Au haut de la côte, qu'il pleuve ou vente, je m'assieds tous les soirs sur un vieux tronc.
25. Les manuscrits D et E sont trop peu anciens pour qu'on puisse en tenir compte.
26. Quelle que soit sa spécialité littéraire originale, il n'est presque plus d'écrivain français aujourd'hui qui n'ait écrit au moins un roman.
27. Malgré les difficultés matérielles, les résultats de la méthode sont assez nombreux pour que l'on puisse dresser un premier bilan.
28. Mais cette pièce, quels que fussent ses mérites éminents, n'avait pas tout à fait la force dramatique et la perfection structurale qu'on admire dans les ouvrages précédents.
29. Un corps solide est un corps dont les distances mutuelles de tous ses points matériels restent invariables, quels que soient son mouvement et les conditions où il se trouve.
30. Quand il s'agit d'un simple *mélange* chimique, les constituants ne perdent pas leur individualité; d'ailleurs on peut les distinguer les uns des autres soit à l'œil nu, soit à la loupe, soit au microscope.

Summary of Uses of Que *and* De; *Words Often Confused*

[1]
Q U E

The French *que* (like English "that") has multiple meanings and deserves close study in the dictionary. Its uses have been presented in various chapters; here they are summarized with the addition of two not previously mentioned.

A] *Que* means "whom," "which," "that" as a relative pronoun; it also appears in the expression *ce que* which means "what" or "which" (see Lesson XI, paragraph 1).

B] *Que* means "what" as an interrogative pronoun (see Lesson XI, paragraph 2).

C] *Que* means "that" as a conjunction.

Il dit que le débit est très faible.	He says (that) the output is very low.
La méthode est si nouvelle qu'on l'ignore.	The method is so new (that) people do not know about it.

As in the case of the relative pronoun, the conjunction *que* does not have to be translated, because "that" is often simply understood.

D] *Que* means "than" or "as" in comparisons. *Plus (moins)* ... *que* means "more (less) ... than"; *aussi ... que* means "as ... as" (see Lesson VIII, paragraph 6d).

Le rendement de la traction à vapeur est moins élevé que celui de la traction électrique.	The efficiency of steam traction is less high than that of electric traction.

Il était plus frivole que n'aurait dû l'être un monsieur si distingué.	He was more frivolous than such a distinguished gentleman should have been.
Son écriture est aussi illisible que la tienne.	His handwriting is as illegible as yours.

Que is followed by inverted word order in the second example. This is common in its use as a conjunction as well as a relative pronoun.

E] *Que* takes on the full meaning of a number of conjunctions when it stands in place of a repetition of the conjunction (see Lesson XII, paragraph 2a and footnote).

Il était triste *parce qu*'on ne l'aimait pas et *qu*'il le savait.	He was sad *because* people did not like him and (*because*) he knew it.
Bien que nous gardions le silence et *que* nous l'exigions de la part des autres...	*Although* we keep silent and *although* we demand silence from the others . . .

When paired with *si*, *que* is followed by a verb in the subjunctive (see Lesson XII, paragraph 2a).

F] *Ne … que* means "only" (see Lesson VI, paragraphs 5 and 6). Review particularly its significance in combination with other negatives; for example, *ne …jamais … que.*

G] *Que … ou (que)…* followed by subjunctives means "whether . . . or (whether) . . . " (see Lesson XIII, paragraph 3c(6)).

Cette propriété appartient à tous les champs magnétiques, qu'ils soient produits par des aimants ou par des courants.	This property belongs to all magnetic fields, whether they are produced by magnets or currents.

H] *Que* means "how" when it introduces exclamatory sentences ending in an adjective or an adverb (see Lesson XIII, paragraph 6).

Qu'il fait beau!	How beautiful the weather is!
Que vous jouez bien!	How well you play!

Comme can be used in the same way (*Comme il fait beau!*).

I] *Que de* means "how many" (= *Combien de*) when introducing exclamatory sentences (see Lesson XIII, paragraph 6).

Que de fois il m'en a parlé!　　How many times he has spoken to
　　　　　　　　　　　　　　　　me about it!

J] *Que* is used with a subjunctive in the main clause to express
the kind of wish that in English is usually introduced by "let" or
"may" (see Lesson XIII, paragraph 4).

Qu'il fasse un effort!　　　　Let him make an effort!
Que Dieu me pardonne!　　　May God forgive me!
Que Votre volonté soit faite!　Thy will be done!

K] *Que ... ne...* means "Why ... not ... " (compare Lesson
VI, paragraph 9b).

Que n'est-il ici?　　　　　　Why is he not here?

L] *Que* (*que de*) is untranslatable when it introduces a noun or
infinitive in apposition.

C'est un sport merveilleux que le　Skiing is a marvelous sport.
　ski.
C'est un mensonge que de dire une　It is a lie to say a thing like that.
　chose pareille.

M] *Que* is used to join the clauses of a conditional sentence
(see Lesson XII, paragraph 2e).

Il le lirait de ses propres yeux, qu'il　If he read it with his own eyes, he
　ne le croirait pas.　　　　　　　would not believe it.

[2]
D E

De, also, has many uses and has been frequently mentioned in
idiomatic constructions cited in preceding chapters. It too can
bear study in the dictionary. Following is a review of its principal
meanings.

A] *De* as a simple preposition means "of" or "from."

la fin du monde　　　　　　the end of the world
Il est venu de Berlin.　　　　He came from Berlin.

B] *De*, with or without the definite article, is used to indicate
the partitive, that is, the French way of expressing "some" or
"any."

Qui a *de* l'essence?	Who has (*some*) gasoline?
Le facteur nous a apporté *des* lettres.	The mailman brought us some letters.
Je n'ai pas *d'*essence.	I haven't *any* gasoline (I have *no* gasoline).
Nous n'avons pas reçu *de* lettres.	We did not receive *any* letters.
Il y a *d'*autres lettres dans votre bureau.	There are (*some*) other letters in your office.
Ce sont *de* vrais intellectuels.	They are real intellectuals.
Avez-vous jamais eu *de* bons étudiants?	Have you ever had (*any*) good students?
beaucoup *de* géographes	many geographers
trop *de* peine	too much trouble
bien *des* Français	many Frenchmen
la plupart *des* géographes	most geographers

De alone is used as the partitive article (1) after negatives, (2) before plural adjectives, (3) after adverbs of quantity (*beaucoup, trop, peu, plus, moins, combien, tant, un peu, assez*; exceptions: *bien des, la plupart des*). All of these uses are illustrated above.

Often the best method of treating the partitive article in translation is to omit it.

Note carefully the difference in meaning of the following pairs of sentences; only the *de* can link the adverb with a noun following it.

Ce petit appareil pratique facilite *beaucoup* ces opérations.	This practical little device *greatly* facilitates these operations.
Ce petit appareil pratique facilite *beaucoup de ces opérations.*	This practical little device facilitates *many of these operations.*
On en souligne *trop* les excuses.	They emphasize the excuses for it *too much.*
On trouve *trop d'excuses* quand on travaille mal.	They offer *too many excuses* when they work poorly.

C] *De* is translated "than" after *plus* (*moins*) followed by a numeral.

On compte aujourd'hui plus de quatre cents volcans actifs.	There are today more than four hundred active volcanoes.

D] *De* denotes "with" or "by" when it shows the means by which the action is accomplished.

Cette usine est munie *de* turbines de 3000 à 4000 chevaux.	This factory is equipped *with* turbines of from 3000 to 4000 horsepower.

| Une île est un espace de terre entourée *d'*eau de tous côtés. | An island is a land area surrounded *by* water on all sides. |

E] *De* means "in" with *façon, manière: de cette façon, d'une autre manière*; "in" or "on" with *côté: de ce côté, de l'autre côté* (see Lesson VI, Idioms).

F] *De* is often best considered as a part of an idiom; for example, *se soucier de, avoir besoin de,* or *se passer de.*

G] *De,* in the following cases, has no English equivalent and must be omitted in translation:

(1) After a noun or an adjective followed by an infinitive.

| Je n'ai guère eu le temps *de* lire le rapport. | I scarcely had time to read the report. |
| Nous sommes enchantés *de* faire votre connaissance. | We are happy to make your acquaintance. |

(2) After certain verbs followed by an infinitive: for example, *essayer* or *refuser.*

| Essayez *de* vous calmer. | Try to calm down. |

The dictionary will always indicate whether a given verb takes *de* before an infinitive. One group takes *à* before an infinitive, and still others take an infinitive directly, as in English.

(3) Between the following pronoun expressions and their adjective modifiers:

quelque chose *d'*intéressant	something interesting
rien *de* nouveau	nothing new
quelqu'un *d'*assez fort	someone strong enough
personne *de* qualifié	nobody qualified
tout ce qui s'écrit *de* plus intéressant	the most interesting things written

[3]
WORDS OFTEN CONFUSED

Study carefully the distinction in meaning of the following groups, which are often misinterpreted by the hasty reader.

le côté; la côte (see Lesson VI, IDIOMS)
la part; la partie; le parti (see Lesson XII, IDIOMS)
partir (note carefully its present tenses and past participle)
le marché market

la marche	step (stairs); running, functioning, operating (machines); march, gait (see Lesson III, IDIOMS)
marcher	to walk; to go, work, function, operate (of machines); to march
deviner	to guess
devenir	to become
dévier	to deviate
monter	to climb, go up, mount
montrer	to show
jouir (de)	to enjoy
jouer	to play; *jouer de* (a musical instrument); *jouer à* (a game)
tuer	to kill
se taire	to be, or become, silent (note carefully its past definite and past participle)
le port	port
la porte	door; gate
la portée	range, scope
porter	to carry, bear (note carefully present tense and past participle)

Distinguish carefully the science or profession from the man practicing it. The items of the second column are those usually misinterpreted. When learning to distinguish between the paired words it helps to pronounce the French words aloud.

THE SCIENCE OR PROFESSION	THE MAN PRACTICING IT
l'agronomie	l'agronome
l'astronomie	l'astronome
la chimie	le chimiste
le génie (*engineering*)	l'ingénieur
(*le génie* also means "genius")	
la géographie	le géographe
la géologie	le géologue
la médecine	le médecin
la philosophie	le philosophe
la photographie (*photography;*	le photographe (*photographer*)
photograph)	
la physique	le physicien
la psychologie	le psychologue
la sociologie	le sociologue

[4]
IRREGULAR VERBS

Review the forms of the irregular verbs *s'asseoir, acquérir, résoudre, boire* in APPENDIX E.

EXERCISES

A. Identify the tense and translate.

1. Je m'assieds.		19. Ils se sont tués.
2. Elles étaient assises.		20. Ils se sont tus.
3. Elles s'étaient assises.		21. Elles ne se sont pas tues.
4. Ils acquéraient.		22. Tues-tu?
5. Acquerrait-il?		23. Ils se turent.
6. Ils acquièrent.		24. Ils se tuent.
7. Ils acquirent.		25. Je ne me suis pas tué.
8. Nous résolvons.		26. Je ne me suis pas tuée.
9. Nous résoudrons.		27. Nous jouions.
10. Nous avions résolu.		28. Nous en jouirons.
11. Il ne but pas.		29. On a acquis.
12. Vous boirez.		30. Nous nous sommes tués.
13. Buviez-vous?		31. Il devine.
14. Elles ont deviné.		32. Il devient.
15. Sont-elles devenues?		33. Ils dévient.
16. Il n'en jouissait pas.		34. Ils deviennent.
17. Ils ne jouent pas.		35. Ils devinent.
18. Ont-ils bu?		

B. Translate.

1. D'autres lettres que les miennes l'auront découragé.
2. Serait-ce trop que de demander de vous voir demain?
3. Il y a trente ans qu'a paru ce volume.
4. C'est une grande curiosité qu'une grenouille.
5. Que le Seigneur ait pitié de nous!
6. Paris est un grand port et les grands navires, arrivant de tous les pays, viennent jusqu'à ses portes.
7. Quoiqu'il aime écrire et qu'il écrive beaucoup, on peut dire que ses livres ne jouissent pas d'une grande popularité.
8. Montez au premier étage et montrez-lui où se trouve la salle de bains.
9. En ne voyant plus mon ancien camarade, j'ai deviné ce qu'il était devenu.
10. Je regrette de dire qu'il est temps de vous quitter.
11. L'hiver, que le temps soit orageux ou non, est toujours ma saison préférée pour travailler.
12. Que de bonnes résolutions il a prises sans s'y tenir.
13. Efforcez-vous de lire de bons livres.
14. Il étudierait le violon douze ans qu'il ne jouerait pas mieux.
15. Le directeur actuel est moins timide que ne l'étaient ses prédécesseurs.
16. Le voleur qu'a blessé le deuxième agent de police n'est pas le même que celui qui a blessé le premier agent.
17. Je me suis souvenu alors de ce que disait le curé à l'enterrement de mon père.
18. Des gens sont venus me voir, de petits propriétaires des environs.
19. Ces rédacteurs peuvent puiser dans ce qui s'écrit de mieux au milieu de la masse de livres et de revues qui se publient. Il s'ensuit donc que tout ce qui s'écrit de plus intéressant à l'heure actuelle est susceptible d'être publié dans leur revue.

20. La plupart des savants ne sont pas des espèces de génies distraits.
21. Les charges électriques peuvent être modifiées de différentes façons.
22. La force électrique est une force à longue portée, c'est-à-dire que son action peut se faire sentir jusqu'à de grandes distances.
23. La mécanique régit le mouvement des corps, quels que soient les phénomènes physiques en cause.
24. Des expériences révélèrent qu'il ne s'agit pas là d'un phénomène accidentel, mais bien d'un moyen de réduire la réflexion de la lumière.
25. L'avenir exige des recherches de plus en plus approfondies : aussi les savants d'aujourd'hui comptent-ils sur les savants de demain.

APPENDIX A

List of French Prepositions, Conjunctions, and Adverbs

FRENCH prepositions, conjunctions, and adverbs are the most difficult words to learn and retain. A systematic effort to memorize them will be rewarded with a marked improvement in reading skill. The following list does not include the common words in this category, except when one meaning is likely to be overlooked in favor of another. An italicized English word indicates an often overlooked meaning. Many of these expressions can also be classified as idioms.

The expressions are not arranged alphabetically because the first words are often not the key words and this list is not primarily intended for quick reference. It has been compiled with a view toward easy memorization: synonyms appearing in sequence (for example, *pourtant*, *cependant*, *toutefois*) and pairs often confused are put together for contrast (*surtout*, *partout*); if these principles do not apply, word families are kept together (*bientôt*, *aussitôt*) or words of greater frequency are presented first.

PREPOSITIONS

1. *à cause de* because of
2. *autour de* around
3. *entre* between; among
4. *parmi* among
5. *chez* at the home of, at the office of; *in the works of*; *in, among*
6. *à côté de* beside, next to
7. *le long de* along
8. *hors de* out of, outside of
9. *du côté de* in the direction of, toward
10. *à partir de* from . . . on (*à partir de 1914*)
11. *dès* from, from . . . on (*dès 1914*), as early as
12. *quant à* as for
13. *d'après* according to
14. *selon* according to
15. *suivant* according to (not to be confused with *suivant* as a present participle)
16. *grâce à* thanks to
17. *afin de* (+inf.) so as to, in order to (=*pour*+inf.)
18. *malgré* in spite of
19. *envers* toward

20. *à la suite de* following
21. *par suite de* in consequence of
22. *outre* beyond, in addition to
23. *à travers* through, across
24. *depuis ... jusqu'à* from . . . to
    . . . *(depuis le plus grand jusqu'au plus petit)*
25. *jusque/jusqu'à* up to, as far as (place); until (time); even
26. *auprès de* close to, near (often indicates a kind of moral relationship which has to be translated into English in a variety of ways according to the particular French idiom)
27. *de manière à* so as to, in such a way as to
28. *à force de* by dint of, by means of
29. *lors de* at the time of
30. *faute de* for lack of
31. *en vue de* so as to, with a view to
32. *en fonction de* in terms of
33. *au-dessus de* above
34. *au-dessous de* below, beneath
35. *au delà de* beyond

CONJUNCTIONS

1. *puisque* since
2. *car* for, because
3. *bien que* although
4. *quoique* although
5. *aussitôt que* as soon as
6. *dès que* as soon as
7. *lorsque* when (=*quand*)
8. *tandis que* whereas, while
9. *alors que* whereas, while
10. *à moins que* unless
11. *pendant que* while
12. *à mesure que (au fur et à mesure que)* as, in proportion to
13. *tant que* as long as (sometimes has its literal meaning "so much that," "so many that")
14. *tant ... que* both . . . and
15. *afin que* so that, in order that (see Preposition List, No. 17)
16. *pour que* so that, in order that
17. *jusqu'à ce que* until (see Preposition List, No. 25)
18. *pourvu que* provided that
19. *de sorte que* so that
20. *si bien que* so that
21. *de même que* in the same way as (in the same way that), just as
22. *ainsi que* as well as; just as
23. *tel que* such as, as, like
24. *en tant que* considered as, as
25. *ou bien* or else
26. *soit ... soit* either . . . or
27. *soit que ... soit que* whether . . . or (whether)
28. *comme* like, as; *as if*; *as it were*
29. *d'autant que* especially since, inasmuch as
30. *d'autant plus (moins) que* all the more (less) because
31. *chaque fois que* whenever
32. *et pourtant* and yet

ADVERBS

1. *d'abord* first, at first
2. *donc* therefore, then (also used as a term of emphasis, rendered in English in a variety of ways)
3. *pourtant* however
4. *cependant* however; *meanwhile*
5. *toutefois* however
6. *néanmoins* nevertheless
7. *or* now
8. *aussi* also; *therefore, so* (when first in the sentence or clause and usually with interrogative word order)
9. *presque* almost

10. *surtout* especially, *chiefly*, above all
11. *partout* everywhere
12. *déjà* already
13. *toujours* always; *still*
14. *encore* still, yet; again (*encore un*, *encore une*, another)
15. *ainsi* thus, in this way, in that way
16. *même* even (as an adjective, however, *même* means "same" before the noun, "very" or "self" after the noun)
17. *assez* enough; *rather*
18. *plutôt* rather
19. *tôt* soon; *early*
20. *bientôt* soon
21. *tantôt ... tantôt* sometimes... sometimes
22. *aussitôt* immediately, at once (see Conjunction List, No. 5)
23. *tout de suite* immediately, at once
24. *tout à coup* suddenly
25. *tout à fait* quite, entirely, completely
26. *tout à l'heure* just a moment ago (with a past tense), in just a moment (with a future tense)
27. *ne ... point* not (*ne ... pas*)
28. *ne ... plus* no longer, no more
29. *ne ... guère* scarcely, hardly
30. *ne ... jamais* never
31. *ne ... que* only
32. *ne ... jamais que* never anything (anybody) but (except)
33. *ne ... guère que* scarcely anything (anybody) but
34. *ne ... plus que* no longer anything (anybody) but, now only
35. *non plus* either (used after a complete negative, e.g. *Paul ne vient pas non plus*); not to be confused with *ne ... plus* (see Lesson VI for all negatives)

36. *jamais* never (when used without a verb), ever (when used with a verb, but without *ne*)
37. *au moins* at least
38. *du moins* at least, at any rate
39. *ailleurs* elsewhere, somewhere else
40. *d'ailleurs* moreover, besides
41. *par ailleurs* moreover, besides; otherwise
42. *de plus* moreover, besides
43. *en outre* moreover, besides (see Preposition Lists, No. 22)
44. *du reste* moreover, besides
45. *autrement* otherwise
46. *de même* in the same way, likewise (see Conjunction List, No. 21)
47. *également* equally, *likewise*
48. *tout de même* just the same, nevertheless
49. *à peu près* nearly, about
50. *à la fois* at the same time
51. *tant* so much, so many
52. *autant* as much, as many
53. *et ainsi de suite* and so forth
54. *à peine* scarcely, hardly (=*ne ... guère*)
55. *davantage* more, further
56. *autrefois* formerly
57. *désormais* henceforth
58. *en quelque sorte* as it were, in a way, in a certain respect
59. *pour ainsi dire* so to speak
60. *sous ce rapport* in this respect
61. *en effet* in fact
62. *d'une part ... d'autre part* on the one hand ... on the other hand
63. *quelque part* somewhere
64. *nulle part* nowhere (see Lesson XII, Idioms, for all expressions with *part*)
65. *d'habitude* usually
66. *comme d'habitude* as usual
67. *de plus en plus* more and more

68. *en somme* in short

69. *à l'étranger* in foreign countries, abroad

70. *à fond* thoroughly

71. *au fond* basically

72. *dès lors* from that moment on, ever since then; consequently

73. *par suite* consequently (see Preposition List, No. 21)

74. *par la suite* subsequently (see Preposition List, No. 20)

75. *là-dessus (là-dessous; là-dedans)* on it, thereon, thereupon (under it; in it, therein)

76. *au fur et à mesure* progressively as, in proportion (see Conjunction List, No. 12)

77. *sans doute* no doubt, probably *(sans aucun doute,* without a doubt)

APPENDIX B

False Cognates

FALSE cognates are French words which look like English words, but which have different or additional meanings. The following list contains the most familiar among them. If the English cognate is acceptable and rather common, it is included among the meanings, but the italicized words indicate other meanings easily overlooked. Memorize them. A few false cognates which have been treated under other headings are not repeated here.

achever *v.* to finish, put the finishing touch to

actuel, actuelle *adj.* current, present; **actuellement** *adv.* at the present time, now, currently

amateur *m.* *lover* (of something), *enthusiast* (**amateur de sports** sports fan); amateur

assister (à) *v.* to attend, be present at; **assistance** *f.* audience, attendance, persons present

blesser *v.* to wound, hurt, injure

chance *f.* *luck*; chance

cloche *f.* bell

conférence *f.* *lecture*; conference

conscience *f.* *consciousness*; conscience

crier *v.* to cry out, shout; **s'écrier** *v.* to exclaim

défendre *v.* to *forbid*; defend; **défense** *f.* *prohibition*; defense (**défense de fumer** smoking prohibited)

dérober *v.* to steal; to conceal

disposer de *v.* to have available, to have at one's disposal

dresser *v.* to erect, put up; to draw up, make out (a report or other document)

embarrassé, embarrassée *adj.* *weighted down, encumbered*; *troubled*; embarrassed; **embarrassant, embarrassante** *adj.* *perplexing*, embarrassing; *troublesome*

employé *m.* *administrative worker, office worker, white-collar worker*; employee

éprouver *v.* to test, try; to experience

esprit *m.* *mind, intelligence*; *wit*; spirit

expérience *f.* *experiment*; experience

faible *adj.* weak, feeble; *low, small* (particularly in technical connotations)

figure *f.* *face, countenance*; figure

force *f.* *strength*, force

formation *f.* formation, *training*; **former** *v.* to form, *train*

hôtel *m.* *private residence, mansion*; hotel (**hôtel de ville** city hall)

ignorer *v.* to be unaware, not to know (= **ne pas savoir**); in more recent usage it sometimes does mean "ignore."

imaginer *v.* *to think up, invent, conceive*; to imagine

inconvénient *m.* disadvantage

injure *f.* insult, insulting remark

instruction *f.* *education*; instruction; **instruire** *v.* to *educate*, instruct; **instruit, instruite** *adj.* *educated, well-educated*

intéressé, intéressée *adj.* interested, *concerned*; *biased*

issue *f.* outlet, way out, solution; outcome

journée *f.* day

large *adj.* broad

lecture *f.* reading

librairie *f.* bookstore

mémoire *f.* memory; *n.m.* *report, memorandum*; **mémoires** memoirs

parent, parente relative

peine *f.* *trouble, difficulty*; pain

perspective *f.* *prospect*; perspective

peuple *m.* *common people, lower classes*; nation, people (for example, **le peuple français**)

pièce *f.* *room*; *play, drama*; piece

place *f.* *public square, plaza*; seat; *room, space*; place

prétendre *v.* to claim, maintain

réaliser *v.* to *achieve*, realize; **réalisation** *f.* *achievement, accomplishment*

rester *v.* to remain

réunion *f.* meeting

sensible *adj.* sensitive (**sensé** sensible, reasonable, showing good sense)

sort *m.* fate (**la sorte** sort, kind)

soumettre *v.* *to subject*; to submit

spirituel, spirituelle *adj.* *witty*; spiritual

tentative *f.* attempt (verb form is tenter, to attempt = essayer; tenter also means "to tempt"; the corresponding noun is **la tentation**) tentatif, tentative *adj.* tentative (to distinguish between the feminine adjective and the noun, go by the position, as explained in Lesson VIII, paragraph 4d)

user *v.* to wear out, use up; **usé, usée** *adj.* worn out; **user de** to use (= **employer, se servir de**)

visiter *v.* to *examine, inspect*; to visit; **la visite** *inspection*; visit

Numerals and Measurement

[1]
CARDINAL NUMBERS

0	zéro	26	vingt-six
1	un, une	27	vingt-sept
2	deux	28	vingt-huit
3	trois	29	vingt-neuf
4	quatre	30	trente
5	cinq	31	trente et un
6	six	32	trente-deux
7	sept	40	quarante
8	huit	50	cinquante
9	neuf	60	soixante
10	dix	70	soixante-dix
11	onze	71	soixante et onze
12	douze	72	soixante-douze
13	treize	73	soixante-treize
14	quatorze	74	soixante-quatorze
15	quinze	75	soixante-quinze
16	seize	76	soixante-seize
17	dix-sept	77	soixante-dix-sept
18	dix-huit	78	soixante-dix-huit
19	dix-neuf	79	soixante-dix-neuf
20	vingt	80	quatre-vingts
21	vingt et un	81	quatre-vingt-un
22	vingt-deux	82	quatre-vingt-deux
23	vingt-trois	90	quatre-vingt-dix
24	vingt-quatre	91	quatre-vingt-onze
25	vingt-cinq	100	cent

1000	mille	1,000,000	un million
2000	deux mille	1,000,000,000	un milliard
3195	trois mille cent quatre-vingt-quinze		

The addition of the ending -aine means approximately that number, except *une douzaine*, which is an exact number. *Mille* follows a different principle.

une dizaine	about ten, some ten, half a score
une vingtaine	about twenty, a score
des centaines	hundreds
une douzaine	a dozen, one dozen
des milliers	thousands

In English commas are used in numbers over three figures; French, however, leaves a space or inserts periods.

1 000 000   1.000.000.

In decimals French substitutes a comma for the English period:

1,5 NF   1.50 New Francs   (A "new" franc is about 20 cents.)

Sur means "out of" when preceded and followed by numbers.

Un Français sur cinq   one Frenchman out of five

[2]
ORDINAL NUMBERS

premier, première	first	*sixième*	sixth
second, seconde;	second	*septième*	seventh
deuxième		*huitième*	eighth
troisième	third	*neuvième*	ninth
quatrième	fourth	*dixième*	tenth
cinquième	fifth	*vingt-deuxième*	twenty-second

[3]
FRACTIONS

le demi, la moitié	half
le tiers	third
le quart	fourth, quarter

Other fractions are formed from the ordinals.

un cinquième   one-fifth

[4]
DIMENSIONS

There are various ways of expressing dimensions in French:

La maison a 15 m de long (longueur).	The house is 15 meters long.
Elle a 8 m de large (largeur).	It is 8 meters wide.
Elle a 6,55 m de haut (hauteur).	It is 6.55 meters high.

They can take the following form:

La maison est longue de 15 m.	The house is 15 meters long.
C'est un objet haut de 3 m.	It is an object 3 meters tall.

Note the meanings of *sur* and *de* in the following:

La maison a 15 m de long sur 8 m de large.	The house is 15 meters long by 8 meters wide.
Elle est plus haute que l'autre de 2 m.	It is 2 meters taller than the other.

[5]
TIME OF DAY

Il est une heure.	It is one o'clock.
Une heure dix.	Ten minutes past one
Une heure et quart	A quarter after one
Une heure vingt	Twenty after one
Une heure et demie	One-thirty, half past one
Deux heures moins dix-huit	Eighteen minutes to two
Deux heures moins le quart	A quarter to two
Deux heures	Two o'clock
Il est midi.	It is twelve noon.
Il est minuit.	It is midnight.
Il est midi et demi.	It is half past twelve.
Six heures du matin	6:00 A.M.
Six heures du soir	6:00 P.M.

[6]
DAYS OF THE WEEK

lundi (*Monday*)	mercredi (*Wednesday*)
mardi (*Tuesday*)	jeudi (*Thursday*)

vendredi   (*Friday*)   dimanche   (*Sunday*)
samedi   (*Saturday*)

[7]
MONTHS OF THE YEAR

janvier	mai	septembre
février	juin	octobre
mars	juillet	novembre
avril	août	décembre

There is nothing quite so indispensable as accurate figures in the work of scientists and technicians. Be particularly careful not to confuse "five" and its multiples (*cinq, quinze, cinquante*), not to misinterpret *un milliard* as *un million*, and not to confuse *le quart* with *quatre*—the most frequent errors in numerals in the work of careless readers.

APPENDIX D

Glossary of Grammatical Terms

Accent   a mark over a French vowel which shows that it is to be pronounced in a certain way (for example, *était, mène, hôte*) or which distinguishes two words otherwise spelled identically (*du, dû; ou, où; la, là*). French uses the acute accent (´), grave accent (`) , and the circumflex (ˆ). Note that these accents have nothing to do with stress.

Adjective   a word that modifies a noun. Notice in the following series that the basic idea "man" is progressively modified by successive addition of adjectives: man; *a* man; *a tall* man; *a tall, distinguished* man; *a tall, distinguished* man *standing* near the window.

Adverb   a word that modifies a verb (they sing *well*), an adjective (they sang a *very* pretty song), or another adverb (they sing *quite* well).

Apposition   a noun in apposition to another noun is one that follows and explains it. EXAMPLE: George, my cousin, is coming.

Auxiliary verb   a helping verb, which, when combined with a part of another verb (for example, the past participle), forms a new tense or a special aspect of a tense: He *has* eaten. It *is* eaten.

Clause   a group of words containing a subject and predicate.

    Main (independent)   one that can stand alone and make sense. EXAMPLE: He spoke quietly.

    Subordinate (dependent)   one that makes sense only when accompanying a main clause. EXAMPLE: because he did not want to disturb anybody.

Comparison   a modification of adjectives and adverbs to show differences of degree. There are three degrees: positive, comparative, and superlative. EXAMPLE: tall, taller, tallest.

Conjugation   a large group of verbs which uses the same combination of stems and endings to express variations in person, number, and tense. There are three regular conjugations in French. Verbs belonging to one of these three conjugations are called regular verbs.

Conjunction   a connective word that indicates the relationship between clauses or other elements of the sentence. EXAMPLES: because, that, and, as.

Demonstrative adjectives and pronouns   words that point out, and in English there are only four: singular, this, that; plural, these, those. They are adjectives if they modify the noun; this book, those persons. They are pronouns if they stand alone: *That* is my book. I like *this*.

Elliptical   leaving something understood. For example, in the following sentence the part in parentheses would usually be understood: I can swim; he cannot (swim).

Gender   in grammar a classification by which nouns and pronouns and sometimes their modifiers are divided according to their sex or lack of it. In English gender is divided naturally into masculine, feminine, and neuter, the neuter being applied to inanimate objects. In French, however, there are only two genders, masculine and feminine, by which even inanimate objects are classified. Sometimes this artificiality of gender may extend to an actual contradiction of the sex of the designee: *la personne, la sentinelle, la grenouille*.

Idiom   a combination of words, peculiar to a particular language, which has a different meaning from that conveyed by a literal translation.

Indirect object   the person *to* or *for* whom an action is undertaken.
   EXAMPLES: I bought *James* a book. I gave *James* the book. I gave the book *to James*. He gave *me* some money. I handed *him* a receipt. In English the preposition may be expressed or understood; in French the preposition is expressed with nouns (*J'ai donné le livre* à Jacques), not with the pronouns (*Je lui ai donné le livre*).

Infinitive   the verb form by which the verb is named or, to put it in other words, the verb form that describes the action without reference to time or person. In English the infinitive is shown by prefixing the word "to"; in French it is shown by the ending (**-er, -ir, -re, -oir**).

Inflection   a variation in the basic form of a word in accordance with a variation in person, gender, number, tense. Compared with French, English has few grammatical inflections left, but one surviving inflection is shown in the third person singular of the present tense: I walk, he walks.

Intransitive   see **Verb**.

Invariable   having only one form which never changes. The French adverb *vite*, for example, is invariable, whereas the adjective *bon, bonne, bons, bonnes* varies to show gender and number.

Mood   the manner in which the action of the verb is stated, namely as a fact (indicative: There *he goes*), as a command (imperative: *Go!*), or as something doubtful or merely desired (subjunctive: I suggest that *he go*).
   Indicative   the mood that treats the action of a verb as a fact stated (*he ran*), denied (*he did not run*), or inquired about (*did he run? didn't he run?*).
   Imperative   giving a command (Come! Sit down! Don't go!) "You" is understood. French uses as imperatives, without any expressed subject, not only the forms that go with *tu* and *vous*, but also with *nous*.
   Subjunctive   see description and examples under "Mood" above and at the beginning of Lesson 13.

Noun   the name of a person or thing. A noun stands as the subject of a sentence, as the object of a verb or preposition, as a predicate complement (my brother is a *lawyer*), or in apposition to explain another noun (Edna, the *secretary*, telephoned me).

Number   the distinction between *one* (singular) and *more than one* (plural). In English number is represented chiefly by nouns and pronouns. The only adjectives to show it are the two demonstratives (*this, these; that, those*); and English verbs show it only in the third person of the present tense (*he speaks; they speak*). In French, however, number is shown by nouns, pronouns, adjectives, and verbs.

Passive voice   the verb form that shows the subject as the receiver of the action: The trash *has been removed* by the haulers. The book *is being* widely *read*. (Active voice: The haulers *have removed* the trash. People *are reading* the book.) In the passive voice the person "by whom" the action is done is called the agent. The agent is not necessarily expressed.

Past participle   the verb form used with "have," "has," or "had": He has *spoken*. This same form can be adapted in both French and English as an adjective: the *spoken* lines; the lines *spoken* by the actor.

Possessive adjectives and pronouns   those that show possession. The possessive adjectives in English are "my," "your," "his," "her," "its," "our," "their." They stand next to a noun: *my* friend, *their* difficulty. The forms "mine," "yours," "his," "hers," "ours," "theirs" are used alone and are pronouns: You take your car, and I'll take *mine*.

Preposition   a short connective word or expression which joins a noun or pronoun to the rest of the sentence and demonstrates its relation. EXAMPLES: with, by, for.

Present participle   the adjectival form of the French verb ending in **-ant** corresponding to the English verb form in **-ing**. In English this same form can be used as a noun, but in French only the infinitive can be so used.

Pronoun   a word that stands in place of a noun; it has meaning only as it refers to a person or thing already mentioned or indicated by the situation. There are various classifications of pronouns according to their functions.

Personal   one that replaces a noun as subject or object: I, me; you; he, him. In French further subdivisions produce conjunctive and disjunctive, as mentioned in Lesson IX. Personal pronouns are almost the only words that retain inflections in English; that is, their forms differ as subject and object: *I* saw *him*. *He* saw *me*. The French forms are inflected even more than English (*see* Lesson IX).

Interrogative   one that is used to ask a question.

Relative   one that joins a subordinate clause to a main clause while at the same time serving as the subject, object, or object of a preposition in the subordinate clause. Relative pronouns in English are "who," "whose," "whom," "which," "that," "what."

Possessive   *see* **Possessive adjectives and pronouns.**

Indefinite   one that does not refer to a definite person or thing: "one," "someone," "something," "whoever."

Reflexive verb   a verb that shows the action turned back on the subject; in other words, an action whose subject and object are the same person or thing: Did you hurt yourself?

Tense   basically, the time (past, present, future) to which a particular verb form refers. There are refinements on this basic division: for example, to describe a past action that occurred before another past action (pluperfect); a past action that was going on when something else happened (imperfect in French, progressive past in English); a future action that will be completed before another future (future perfect).

Simple   a verb consisting of just one word: Il *dit*. He *says*.

Compound   a tense composed of a helping verb and a past participle: Il *est resté*. He *has stayed*.

Perfect   the word "perfect," used in a grammatical sense, means "complete." It does not refer to perfection. The perfect tenses are those that emphasize the completion of the action.

Imperfect   in French, a past tense that shows action in progress, as habitual in the past, or that describes in the past. Imperfect means "incomplete" in this usage.

Transitive   *see* **Verb.**

Verb   the principal element of the predicate which affirms something about the subject. EXAMPLES: James *left*. James *had left* earlier.

Impersonal   one whose subject is not a person. It appears only in the third person singular and has as its subject "it" or, in French, *il*.

Regular   one that shares the pattern of grammatical inflections of a large number of other verbs. The groups of regular verbs are called regular conjugations.

Irregular   one that does not conform to any of the three regular conjugations. It has a pattern of grammatical inflections all its own, or it shares its pattern with only a few other verbs.

Transitive   one that takes a direct object or one whose action is performed directly on a person or thing. EXAMPLES: I sent the letter. He called me.

Intransitive   one that does not take a direct object. EXAMPLES: He ran. They came down.

APPENDIX E

Conjugation of French Verbs

A LARGE majority of French verbs fall into three patterns or conjugations. These three groupings, in each of which the stems and endings combine according to a predictable formula, are called the three regular conjugations. One model verb for each of them can serve as the pattern for all the hundreds or thousands in that conjugation. Any verb that deviates from these three patterns is classified as irregular and has to be learned individually, at least insofar as it deviates.

A regular verb has five principal parts from which all the forms can be derived. These parts are listed here and illustrated by the three conjugations.

	FIRST CONJUGATION	SECOND CONJUGATION	THIRD CONJUGATION
INFINITIVE	donner	finir	vendre
PRESENT PARTICIPLE	donnant	finissant	vendant
PAST PARTICIPLE	donné	fini	vendu
PRESENT	je donne	je finis	je vends
PAST DEFINITE	je donnai	je finis	je vendis

FORMATION OF THE VARIOUS TENSES FROM THE PRINCIPAL PARTS

A]

The *infinitive* is the stem for the FUTURE and CONDITIONAL.

The FUTURE is formed with the complete infinitive + the endings **-ai, -as, -a, -ons, -ez, -ont.**

The CONDITIONAL is the complete infinitive + **-ais, -ais, -ait, -ions, -iez, -aient.**

Note: Third conjugation verbs drop the **e** of the infinitive ending **-re.**

B]

The *present participle* provides the stem for the IMPERFECT IN-
DICATIVE, the PRESENT SUBJUNCTIVE, and the plural of the
PRESENT INDICATIVE and IMPERATIVE.

The IMPERFECT is formed by the participial stem (*donn-*, *finiss-*,
vend-) and the endings **-ais, -ais, -ait, -ions, -iez, -aient.**

The PRESENT SUBJUNCTIVE is derived from the participial stem
and the endings **-e, -es, -e, -ions, -iez, -ent.**

The plural of the PRESENT INDICATIVE is the participial stem to
which is added the endings **-ons, -ez, -ent**; the first two of
these forms are also used as imperatives.

C]

The *past participle* is combined with the auxiliary *avoir* or *être* to
form all the compound tenses: five indicative compound
tenses, two subjunctive compound tenses, and the PERFECT
INFINITIVE and PERFECT PARTICIPLE. *Avoir* is the auxiliary used
for most verbs (see Lessons I and IV). For every simple verb
tense there is a compound tense which is a combination of the
simple tense of the auxiliary and the past participle: for
example,

IMPERFECT	PLUPERFECT
je donnais	*j'avais donné*

(imperfect of *avoir* and the past participle of *donner*). In the
following pages the paradigms of the regular verbs are
arranged to show the relation of simple and compound tenses.

The *past participle* is also used with *être* to form the passive voice
of transitive verbs (which in the active are conjugated with
avoir).

L'enfant est puni.	The child is punished.
L'enfant a été puni.	The child was (has been) punished.

This is exactly like the English use of "to be" for the same purpose (see Lesson IV, paragraph 6). There is no overlapping
with the verbs that use *être* to form compound tenses because
these verbs (reflexives, intransitives) have no passive voice.

D]

The *present* tense, singular, is the fourth principal part: **donne-,
-es, -e; finis, -is, -it; vends, -s, -** (only *rompre*, of the third

conjugation, adds a -t in the third person: *il rompt*). The familiar singular of the imperative also comes from this stem.

E]

The *past definite*, the fifth principal part, serves also as the stem for the IMPERFECT SUBJUNCTIVE.

The PAST DEFINITE endings of the first conjugation are **donnai, -as, -a, -âmes, -âtes, -èrent;** the second and third conjugations are identical: **finis, -is, -it, -îmes, -îtes, -irent; vendis, -is, -it, -îmes, -îtes, -irent.**

The IMPERFECT SUBJUNCTIVE can be formed by dropping the last letter (*donnai̸, fini̸, vendi̸*) of the PAST DEFINITE and adding the endings: **-sse, -sses, -ˆt, -ssions, -ssiez, -ssent.**

VERB TABLES: REGULAR CONJUGATIONS

Verb tables for the three regular conjugations are located on the next two pairs of facing pages (pp. 126–129).

FIRST CONJUGATION:

PRINCIPAL PARTS: (1) donner, (2) donnant,

———— I N D I C A T I V E ————

PRESENT [4, 2]* (I give, am giving)	IMPERFECT [2] (I was giving, used to give, gave)	PAST DEFINITE [5] (I gave)	FUTURE [1] (I will give, shall give)
je donne [4]	je donnais	je donnai	je donnerai
tu donnes [4]	tu donnais	tu donnas	tu donneras (you
il donne [4]	il donnait	il donna	will give)
nous donnons [2]	nous donnions	nous donnâmes	il donnera
vous donnez [2]	vous donniez	vous donnâtes	nous donnerons
ils donnent [2]	ils donnaient	ils donnèrent	vous donnerez
			ils donneront

PAST INDEFINITE [3] (I gave, have given)	PLUPERFECT [3] (I had given)	PAST ANTERIOR [3] (I had given)	FUTURE PERFECT [3] (I will have given)
j'ai donné	j'avais donné	j'eus donné	j'aurai donné
tu as donné	tu avais donné	tu eus donné	tu auras donné
il a donné	il avait donné	il eut donné	il aura donné
nous avons donné	nous avions donné	nous eûmes donné	nous aurons donné
vous avez donné	vous aviez donné	vous eûtes donné	vous aurez donné
ils ont donné	ils avaient donné	ils eurent donné	ils auront donné

PERFECT INFINITIVE: avoir donné[3] (to have given)
PERFECT PARTICIPLE: ayant donné[3] (having given)

FIRST CONJUGATION:

PRINCIPAL PARTS: (1) arriver, (2) arrivant,

[The five simple tenses are omitted because they follow the pattern for *donner*.]

PAST INDEFINITE [3]* (I arrived, have arrived)	PLUPERFECT [3] (I had arrived)	PAST ANTERIOR [3] (I had arrived)	FUTURE PERFECT [3] (I will have arrived)
je suis arrivé(e)	j'étais arrivé(e)	je fus arrivé(e)	je serai arrivé(e)
tu es arrivé(e)	tu étais arrivé(e)	tu fus arrivé(e)	tu seras arrivé(e)
il est arrivé	il était arrivé	il fut arrivé	il sera arrivé
elle est arrivée	elle était arrivée	elle fut arrivée	elle sera arrivée
nous sommes arrivé(e)s	nous étions arrivé(e)s	nous fûmes arrivé(e)s	nous serons arrivé(e)s
vous êtes arrivé(e)(s)	vous étiez arrivé(e)(s)	vous fûtes arrivé(e)(s)	vous serez arrivé(e)(s)
ils sont arrivés	ils étaient arrivés	ils furent arrivés	ils seront arrivés
elles sont arrivées	elles étaient arrivées	elles furent arrivées	elles seront arrivées

* The numerals indicate from which of the principal parts the tense is derived.

PERFECT INFINITIVE: être arrivé(e)(s)[3] (to have arrived)
PERFECT PARTICIPLE: étant arrivé(e)(s)[3] (having arrived)

DONNER
(3) donné, (4) je donne, (5) je donnai

| | IMPERATIVE | — SUBJUNCTIVE —|

CONDITIONAL [1]
(*I would give*)

PRESENT [2]

IMPERFECT [5]

je donnerais		je donne	je donnasse
tu donnerais	donne(s) [4] (*give*)	tu donnes	tu donnasses
il donnerait		il donne	il donnât
nous donnerions	donnons [2] (*let us give*)	nous donnions	nous donnassions
vous donneriez	donnez [2] (*give*)	vous donniez	vous donnassiez
ils donneraient		ils donnent	ils donnassent

(The singular familiar form adds an -s when followed by *y* or *en*: *marches-y, donnes-en*.)

CONDITIONAL PERFECT [3]
(*I would have given*)

PERFECT [3]

PLUPERFECT [3]

j'aurais donné	j'aie donné	j'eusse donné
tu aurais donné	tu aies donné	tu eusses donné
il aurait donné	il ait donné	il eût donné
nous aurions donné	nous ayons donné	nous eussions donné
vous auriez donné	vous ayez donné	vous eussiez donné
ils auraient donné	ils aient donné	ils eussent donné

ARRIVER (*conjugated with* être)
(3) arrivé, (4) j'arrive, (5) j'arrivai

[The imperative of *arriver* follows the pattern for *donner*.]

[The two simple tenses of the subjunctive of *arriver* are omitted because they follow the pattern given for *donner*.]

CONDITIONAL PERFECT [3]
(*I would have arrived*)

PERFECT [3]

PLUPERFECT [3]

je serais arrivé(e)	je sois arrivé(e)	je fusse arrivé(e)
tu serais arrivé(e)	tu sois arrivé(e)	tu fusses arrivé(e)
il serait arrivé	il soit arrivé	il fût arrivé
elle serait arrivée	elle soit arrivée	elle fût arrivée
nous serions arrivé(e)s	nous soyons arrivé(e)s	nous fussions arrivé(e)s
vous seriez arrivé(e)(s)	vous soyez arrivé(e)(s)	vous fussiez arrivé(e)(s)
ils seraient arrivés	ils soient arrivés	ils fussent arrivés
elles seraient arrivées	elles soient arrivées	elles fussent arrivées

The meanings of the subjunctive forms are treated in Lesson XIII and in Lesson XII, paragraph 2a, 2d, 2g.

SECOND CONJUGATION:

PRINCIPAL PARTS: (1) finir, (2) finissant,

INDICATIVE

PRESENT [4,2] (I finish, am finishing)	IMPERFECT [2] (I was finishing, used to finish, finished)	PAST DEFINITE [5] (I finished)	FUTURE [1] (I will finish, shall finish)
je finis [4]	je finissais	je finis	je finirai
tu finis [4]	tu finissais	tu finis	tu finiras (you will finish)
il finit [4]	il finissait	il finit	il finira
nous finissons [2]	nous finissions	nous finîmes	nous finirons
vous finissez [2]	vous finissiez	vous finîtes	vous finirez
ils finissent [2]	ils finissaient	ils finirent	ils finiront

PAST INDEFINITE [3] (I finished, have finished)	PLUPERFECT [3] (I had finished)	PAST ANTERIOR [3] (I had finished)	FUTURE PERFECT [3] (I will have finished)
j'ai fini (&c.)	j'avais fini (&c.)	j'eus fini (&c.)	j'aurai fini (&c.)

PERFECT INFINITIVE: avoir fini[3] (to have finished)
PERFECT PARTICIPLE: ayant fini[3] (having finished)

THIRD CONJUGATION:

PRINCIPAL PARTS: (1) vendre, (2) vendant,

INDICATIVE

PRESENT [4,2] (I sell, am selling)	IMPERFECT [2] (I was selling, used to sell, sold)	PAST DEFINITE [5] (I sold)	FUTURE [1] (I will sell, shall sell)
je vends [4]	je vendais	je vendis	je vendrai
tu vends [4]	tu vendais	tu vendis	tu vendras (you will sell)
il vend [4]	il vendait	il vendit	il vendra
nous vendons [2]	nous vendions	nous vendîmes	nous vendrons
vous vendez [2]	vous vendiez	vous vendîtes	vous vendrez
ils vendent [2]	ils vendaient	ils vendirent	ils vendront

PAST INDEFINITE [3] (I sold, have sold)	PLUPERFECT [3] (I had sold)	PAST ANTERIOR [3] (I had sold)	FUTURE PERFECT [3] (I will have sold)
j'ai vendu (&c.)	j'avais vendu (&c.)	j'eus vendu (&c.)	j'aurai vendu (&c.)

PERFECT INFINITIVE: avoir vendu[3] (to have sold)
PERFECT PARTICIPLE: ayant vendu[3] (having sold)

FINIR

(3) fini, (4) je finis, (5) je finis

CONDITIONAL [1]	IMPERATIVE [4,2]		— SUBJUNCTIVE —	
(I would finish)			PRESENT [2]	IMPERFECT [5]
je finirais			je finisse	je finisse
tu finirais	finis [4]	(finish)	tu finisses	tu finisses
il finirait			il finisse	il finît
nous finirions	finissons [2]	(let us	nous finissions	nous finissions
vous finiriez		finish)	vous finissiez	vous finissiez
ils finiraient	finissez [2]	(finish)	ils finissent	ils finissent

CONDITIONAL PERFECT [3]	PERFECT [3]	PLUPERFECT [3]
(I would have finished)		
j'aurais fini (&c.)	j'aie fini (&c.)	j'eusse fini (&c.)

VENDRE

(3) vendu, (4) je vends, (5) je vendis

CONDITIONAL [1]	IMPERATIVE [4,2]		— SUBJUNCTIVE —	
(I would sell)			PRESENT [2]	IMPERFECT [5]
je vendrais			je vende	je vendisse
tu vendrais	vends [4]	(sell)	tu vendes	tu vendisses
il vendrait			il vende	il vendît
nous vendrions	vendons [2]	(let's sell)	nous vendions	nous vendissions
vous vendriez	vendez [2]	(sell)	nous vendiez	vous vendissiez
ils vendraient			ils vendent	ils vendissent

CONDITIONAL PERFECT [3]	PERFECT [3]	PLUPERFECT [3]
(I would have sold)		
j'aurais vendu (&c.)	j'aie vendu (&c.)	j'eusse vendu (&c.)

ORTHOGRAPHICAL CHANGES

Some verbs that are not classified as irregular display certain spelling adjustments. Most of them are regular in sound.

[1]
VERBS ENDING -CER OR -GER IN THE INFINITIVE

A] If an infinitive ends in **-cer**, the *c* becomes *ç* before endings beginning with **a** or **o**, in order to retain the [s] sound:

tracer   *je trace*   *nous traçons*   *je traçais*

Compare retention of *e* in "traceable" but not in "tracing" in English.

B] If an infinitive ends in **-ger**, an *e* is inserted before endings beginning with **a** or **o** to retain the soft sound of the *g* in the infinitive.

manger   *je mange*   *nous mangeons*   *je mangeais*

Compare retention of *e* in "manageable" but not in "managing" in English.

[2]
VERBS ENDING IN -YER IN THE INFINITIVE

Verbs ending in **-oyer**, **-uyer**, and **-ayer** change *y* to *i* before a mute *e*, that is, in the present indicative (four endings), the familiar singular imperative, the present subjunctive (four endings), and the entire future and conditional:

EMPLOYER	ESSUYER	ESSAYER
j'emploie	j'essuie	j'essaie
nous employons	nous essuyons	nous essayons
j'emploierai	j'essuierai	j'essaierai

In verbs whose infinitive ends in **-ayer**, the *y* is sometimes retained.
Compare "fly," "flies" in English.

[3]

Verbs with a mute *e* or an *é* in the final syllable of the stem open it up to an è [ɛ] sound when the next syllable contains a mute *e*. This is shown in the spelling either by adding a grave accent to the *e* or by doubling the following consonant. The tenses affected are the present indicative, present subjunctive, imperative, future, and conditional.

MENER	mène	mène	mènerai	mènerais
	mènes	mènes	mèneras	mènerais
	mène	mène	mènera	mènerait
	menons	menions	mènerons	mènerions
	menez	meniez	mènerez	mèneriez
	mènent	mènent	mèneront	mèneraient
APPELER	appelle	appelle	appellerai	appellerais
	appelles	appelles	appelleras	appellerais
	appelle	appelle	appellera	appellerait
	appelons	appelions	appellerons	appellerions
	appelez	appeliez	appellerez	appelleriez
	appellent	appellent	appelleront	appelleraient
JETER	jette	jette	jetterai	jetterais
	jettes	jettes	jetteras	jetterais
	jette	jette	jettera	jetterait
	jetons	jetions	jetterons	jetterions
	jetez	jetiez	jetterez	jetteriez
	jettent	jettent	jetteront	jetteraient

Most verbs ending in **-eler** and **-eter** follow the pattern of *appeler* and *jeter*, but a few follow the pattern of *mener*:

acheter   j'achète   geler   je gèle

Verbs having *é* in the final syllable of the infinitive stem change it to *è* before a mute *e* in the next syllable of the present indicative and present subjunctive, but do not change in the future and conditional.

espérer   j'espère   j'espérerai   j'espérerais

IRREGULAR VERBS

After *avoir* and *être*, which are presented first, alphabetical order is observed for the remainder of the irregular verbs. The five principal parts of each verb are shown, as are any irregular forms. If a tense is not mentioned separately, assume that it is derived in routine fashion from one of the five principal parts, as explained in the introductory pages of Appendix E. No one should start using these tables without being in thorough command of those pages.

1. *AVOIR* TO HAVE

1 *avoir*	2 *ayant*	3 *eu*	4 *j'ai*	5 *j'eus*
FUTURE (*I will have*) j'aurai [&c.] CONDITIONAL (*I would have*) j'aurais [&c.]	IMPERFECT (*I had, used to have*) j'avais [&c.] PRESENT SUBJUNCTIVE j'aie tu aies il ait nous ayons vous ayez ils aient	PAST INDEFINITE (*I had, have had*) j'ai eu [&c.] PLUPERFECT (*I had had*) j'avais eu [&c.] PAST ANTERIOR (*I had had*) j'eus eu [&c.] FUTURE PERFECT (*I will have had*) j'aurai eu [&c.] CONDITIONAL PERFECT (*I would have had*) j'aurais eu[&c.] PERFECT SUBJUNCTIVE j'aie eu [&c.] PLUPERFECT SUBJUNCTIVE j'eusse eu [&c.]	(*I have*) j'ai tu as il a nous avons vous avez ils ont IMPERATIVE aie (*have*) ayons (*let us have*) ayez (have)	(*I had*) j'eus [&c.] IMPERFECT SUBJUNCTIVE j'eusse [&c.]

¹ The spelling variations described for the regular verbs (Orthographical Changes, pages 130–131) also apply to the irregular verbs which have similar vowel and consonant combinations.

² The plural of the present tense should, strictly speaking, be listed under the present participle, to which stem it usually corresponds, but it is put here in continuation of the singular as a matter of convenience.

2. ETRE [TO BE]

1 être	2 étant	3 été	4 je suis	5 je fus
FUTURE (*I will be*) je serai [&c.]	IMPERFECT (*I was, used to be*) j'étais [&c.]	PAST INDEFINITE (*I was, have been*) j'ai été [&c.]	(*I am*) je suis tu es il est nous sommes vous êtes ils sont	(*I was*) je fus [&c.] IMPERFECT SUBJUNCTIVE je fusse [&c.]
CONDITIONAL (*I would be*) je serais [&c.]	PRESENT SUBJUNCTIVE je sois tu sois il soit nous soyons vous soyez ils soient	PLUPERFECT (*I had been*) j'avais été [&c.] PAST ANTERIOR (*I had been*) j'eus été [&c.]	IMPERATIVE sois (*be*) soyons (*let us be*) soyez (*be*)	

FUTURE
PERFECT
(*I will have been*)
j'aurai été [&c.]

CONDITIONAL
PERFECT
(*I would have
been*)
j'aurais été [&c.]

PERFECT
SUBJUNCTIVE
j'aie été   [&c.]

PLUPERFECT
SUBJUNCTIVE
j'eusse été [&c.]

3. ACQUERIR [TO ACQUIRE]

1 acquérir	2 acquérant	3 acquis	4 j'acquiers	5 j'acquis
FUTURE j'acquerrai	PRESENT SUBJUNCTIVE j'acquière[1] tu acquières il acquière nous acquérions vous acquériez ils acquièrent	PAST INDEFINITE j'ai acquis	j'acquiers tu acquiers il acquiert nous acquérons[1,2] vous acquérez ils acquièrent	

LIKE *Acquérir*: *conquérir*, to conquer

Footnotes for 1 and 2 above appear on facing page.

4. *ALLER* [TO GO]

1 aller	2 allant	3 allé	4 je vais	5 j'allai
FUTURE j'irai	PRESENT SUBJUNCTIVE j'aille tu ailles il aille nous allions vous alliez ils aillent	PAST INDEFINITE je suis allé(e) [1]	je vais tu vas il va nous allons vous allez ils vont IMPERATIVE va* *Va adds the s in the same circumstances as verbs of the first conjugation (see the imperative of *donner*).	

5. *ASSEOIR* [TO SEAT]

1 asseoir	2 asseyant	3 assis	4 j'assieds	5 j'assis
FUTURE j'assiérai		PAST INDEFINITE j'ai assis (je me suis assis)	j'assieds tu assieds il assied nous asseyons vous asseyez ils asseyent	

Except for its participle, used as an adjective (*il est assis*, he is seated [sitting]), this verb appears more frequently as the reflexive *s'asseoir*, to sit down.
Note: There are less frequent alternate forms in -oi- and -ey-.

6. *BATTRE* [TO BEAT]

1 battre	2 battant	3 battu	4 je bats	5 je battis
		PAST INDEFINITE j'ai battu	je bats tu bats il bat nous battons vous battez ils battent	

LIKE *Battre*: *se battre*, to fight

---

[1] For the agreement of past participles in the compound tenses of verbs conjugated with *être* see the example of *arriver* in the Verb Tables of the Regular Conjugations.

7. BOIRE [TO DRINK]

1 boire	2 buvant	3 bu	4 je bois	5 je bus
	PRESENT SUBJUNCTIVE je boive tu boives il boive nous buvions vous buviez ils boivent	PAST INDEFINITE j'ai bu	je bois tu bois il boit nous buvons vous buvez ils boivent	

8. CONCLURE [TO CONCLUDE]

1 conclure	2 concluant	3 conclu	4 je conclus	5 je conclus
		PAST INDEFINITE j'ai conclu	je conclus tu conclus il conclut nous concluons vous concluez ils concluent	

LIKE *Conclure*: *exclure*, to exclude

9. CONDUIRE [TO CONDUCT; DRIVE (an automobile)]

1 conduire	2 conduisant	3 conduit	4 je conduis	5 je conduisis
		PAST INDEFINITE j'ai conduit	je conduis tu conduis il conduit nous con- duisons vous conduisez ils conduisent	

LIKE *Conduire*

construire	to build	*produire*	to produce
détruire	to destroy	*réduire*	to reduce
instruire	to instruct	*traduire*	to translate
introduire	to introduce		

10. *CONNAÎTRE* [TO KNOW, BE ACQUAINTED WITH]

1 connaître	2 connaissant	3 connu	4 je connais	5 je connus
		PAST INDEFINITE j'ai connu	je connais tu connais il connaît nous connaissons vous connaissez ils connaissent	

LIKE *Connaître*

reconnaître	to recognize	*apparaître*	to appear (come into view)
paraître	to appear (seem)	*disparaître*	to disappear

11. *COUDRE* [TO SEW]

1 coudre	2 cousant	3 cousu	4 je couds	5 je cousus
		PAST INDEFINITE j'ai cousu	je couds tu couds il coud nous cousons vous cousez ils cousent	

12. *COURIR* [TO RUN]

1 courir	2 courant	3 couru	4 je cours	5 je courus
FUTURE je courrai		PAST INDEFINITE j'ai couru	je cours tu cours il court nous courons vous courez ils courent	

LIKE *Courir*

accourir	to run up, hasten	*secourir*	to help
parcourir	to run over, go through		

13. CRAINDRE [TO FEAR]

1 *craindre*	2 *craignant*	3 *craint*	4 *je crains*	5 *je craignis*
		PAST INDEFINITE j'ai craint	je crains tu crains il craint nous craignons vous craignez ils craignent	

LIKE *Craindre*

contraindre	to constrain	*peindre*	to paint
plaindre	to pity	*restreindre*	to restrict, limit
se plaindre	to complain	*teindre*	to dye
atteindre	to attain	*joindre*	to join
éteindre	to extinguish	*poindre*	to dawn
feindre	to feign		

14. CROIRE [TO BELIEVE, THINK]

1 *croire*	2 *croyant*	3 *cru*	4 *je crois*	5 *je crus*
	PRESENT SUBJUNCTIVE je croie* tu croies il croie nous croyions vous croyiez ils croient	PAST INDEFINITE j'ai cru	je crois tu crois il croit nous croyons vous croyez ils croient*	

* The *y* of the participial stem changes to *i* before an ending beginning with mute *e* (see paragraph 2 of Orthographical Changes for regular verbs).

15. CROITRE [TO GROW]

1 *croître*	2 *croissant*	3 *crû*	4 *je croîs*	5 *je crûs*
		PAST INDEFINITE j'ai crû	je croîs tu croîs il croît nous croissons vous croissez ils croissent	

The circumflex is added to forms of *croître* to distinguish them from like forms of *croire* except when both have it as a part of the ending (*crûmes, crûtes, crût*).

16. CUEILLIR [TO GATHER, PICK]

1 *cueillir*	2 *cueillant*	3 *cueilli*	4 *je cueille*	5 *je cueillis*
FUTURE je cueillerai		PAST INDEFINITE j'ai cueilli	je cueille tu cueilles il cueille nous cueillons vous cueillez ils cueillent	

LIKE *Cueillir*

accueillir to welcome   *tressaillir* to tremble
                              (has a regular future)

17. DEVOIR [TO OWE; MUST, HAVE TO, OUGHT]

1 *devoir*	2 *devant*	3 *dû (due)*	4 *je dois*	5 *je dus*
FUTURE je devrai	PRESENT SUBJUNCTIVE je doive tu doives il doive nous devions vous deviez ils doivent	PAST INDEFINITE j'ai dû	je dois tu dois il doit nous devons vous devez ils doivent	

18. DIRE [TO SAY, TELL]

1 *dire*	2 *disant*	3 *dit*	4 *je dis*	5 *je dis*
		PAST INDEFINITE j'ai dit	je dis tu dis il dit nous disons vous dites ils disent	

LIKE *Dire*

contredire to contradict   *prédire* to predict
médire   to slander
(However, the 2d pers. pl. present of these compounds ends in -disez)

19. ECRIRE [TO WRITE]

1 écrire	2 écrivant	3 écrit	4 j'écris	5 j'écrivis
		PAST INDEFINITE	j'écris	
		j'ai écrit	tu écris	
			il écrit	
			nous écrivons	
			vous écrivez	
			ils écrivent	

LIKE Ecrire: décrire, to describe, inscrire, to inscribe, register, and all other compounds of écrire.

20. ENVOYER [TO SEND]

1 envoyer	2 envoyant	3 envoyé	4 j'envoie	5 j'envoyai
FUTURE	SUBJUNCTIVE	PAST INDEFINITE	j'envoie	
j'enverrai	j'envoie*	j'ai envoyé	tu envoies	
	tu envoies		il envoie	
	il envoie		nous envoyons	
	nous envoyions		vous envoyez	
	vous envoyiez		ils envoient	
	ils envoient			

* The *y* of the stem changes to *i* before endings containing a mute *e* (see Orthographical Changes, paragraph 2).

21. FAIRE [TO MAKE, TO DO]

1 faire	2 faisant	3 fait	4 je fais	5 je fis
FUTURE	PRESENT SUBJUNCTIVE	PAST INDEFINITE	je fais	
je ferai	je fasse	j'ai fait	tu fais	
	tu fasses		il fait	
	il fasse		nous faisons	
	nous fassions		vous faites	
	vous fassiez		ils font	
	ils fassent			

LIKE Faire: défaire, to undo, satisfaire, to satisfy.

22. FALLOIR [MUST (*impers.*)]

1 *falloir*	2	3 *fallu*	4 *il faut*	5 *il fallut*
FUTURE il faudra	IMPERFECT il fallait PRESENT SUBJUNCTIVE il faille	PAST INDEFINITE il a fallu		

23. FUIR [TO FLEE]

1 *fuir*	2 *fuyant*	3 *fui*	4 *je fuis*	5 *je fuis*
	PRESENT SUBJUNCTIVE je fuie* tu fuies il fuie nous fuyions vous fuyiez ils fuient	PAST INDEFINITE j'ai fui	je fuis tu fuis il fuit nous fuyons vous fuyez ils fuient*	

* The *y* of the present participle changes to *i* before a mute *e* in the ending (see paragraph 2 of Orthographical Changes).

24. LIRE [TO READ]

1 *lire*	2 *lisant*	3 *lu*	4 *je lis*	5 *je lus*
		PAST INDEFINITE j'ai lu	je lis tu lis il lit nous lisons vous lisez ils lisent	

LIKE *Lire*: *élire*, to elect

25. METTRE [TO PUT, PLACE]

1 *mettre*	2 *mettant*	3 *mis*	4 *je mets*	5 *je mis*
		PAST INDEFINITE j'ai mis	je mets tu mets il met nous mettons vous mettez ils mettent	

LIKE *Mettre*

admettre	to admit	*promettre*	to promise
commettre	to commit	*soumettre*	to subject
permettre	to permit		

and all the other compounds of *mettre*.

26. *MOURIR* [TO DIE]

1 *mourir*	2 *mourant*	3 *mort*	4 *je meurs*	5 *je mourus*
FUTURE je mourrai	PRESENT SUBJUNCTIVE je meure tu meures il meure nous mourions vous mouriez ils meurent	PAST INDEFINITE je suis mort(e)	je meurs tu meurs il meurt nous mourons vous mourez ils meurent	

27. *NAITRE* [TO BE BORN]

1 *naître*	2 *naissant*	3 *né*	4 *je nais*	5 *je naquis*
		PAST INDEFINITE je suis né(e)	je nais tu nais il naît nous naissons vous naissez ils naissent	

LIKE *Naître*: *renaître*, to be born again

28. *OUVRIR* [TO OPEN]

1 *ouvrir*	2 *ouvrant*	3 *ouvert*	4 *j'ouvre*	5 *j'ouvris*
		PAST INDEFINITE j'ai ouvert	j'ouvre tu ouvres il ouvre nous ouvrons vous ouvrez ils ouvrent	

LIKE *Ouvrir*

couvrir	to cover	*offrir*	to offer
découvrir	to discover	*souffrir*	to suffer

These verbs all have in common the irregular past participle which ends in **-ert** and the present participle and present tense which follow the pattern for the first conjugation instead of the second conjugation, as the infinitive might indicate.

29. PARTIR [TO LEAVE, SET OUT]

1 partir	2 partant	3 parti	4 je pars	5 je partis
		PAST INDEFINITE je suis parti(e)	je pars tu pars il part nous partons vous partez ils partent	

LIKE *Partir*

consentir	to consent		sentir	to feel
dormir	to sleep		servir	to serve
mentir	to lie		sortir	to go out, come out
se repentir	to repent			

In this list and in all similar verbs irregularities show that the present participial stem does not conform to the second conjugation, as the first, third, and fifth parts do, and that the present tense singular is formed by dropping the last *three* letters of the infinitive before adding the endings -s, -s, -t (*je consens, je dors, je mens, je me repens, je sens, je sers, je sors*).

Bouillir can also be classified with the *partir* verbs if the -ill- is considered to be the final sound, which is dropped in the singular present indicative and imperative: *je bous*, etc.

30. PLAIRE [TO PLEASE]

1 plaire	2 plaisant	3 plu	4 je plais	5 je plus
		PAST INDEFINITE j'ai plu	je plais tu plais il plaît nous plaisons vous plaisez ils plaisent	

LIKE *Plaire*: *se taire*, to be silent, to become silent (except in third person singular present indicative *il se tait* without a circumflex).

31. PLEUVOIR [TO RAIN (*impers.*)]

1 pleuvoir	2 pleuvant	3 plu	4 il pleut	5 il plut
FUTURE il pleuvra		PAST INDEFINITE il a plu		

32. POUVOIR [to be able]

1 pouvoir	2 pouvant	3 pu	4 je peux	5 je pus
FUTURE je pourrai	PRESENT SUBJUNCTIVE je puisse tu puisses il puisse nous puissions vous puissiez ils puissent		je peux (OR je puis) tu peux il peut nous pouvons vous pouvez ils peuvent	

33. PRENDRE [to take]

1 prendre	2 prenant	3 pris	4 je prends	5 je pris
	PRESENT SUBJUNCTIVE je prenne tu prennes il prenne nous prenions vous preniez ils prennent	PAST INDEFINITE j'ai pris	je prends tu prends il prend nous prenons vous prenez ils prennent	

LIKE Prendre

apprendre — to learn
comprendre — to understand; to include
entreprendre — to undertake

surprendre — to surprise, and all other compounds

34. RECEVOIR [to receive]

1 recevoir	2 recevant	3 reçu	4 je reçois	5 je reçus
FUTURE je recevrai	PRESENT SUBJUNCTIVE je reçoive tu reçoives il reçoive nous recevions vous receviez ils reçoivent	PAST INDEFINITE j'ai reçu	je reçois tu reçois il reçoit nous recevons vous recevez ils reçoivent	

LIKE Recevoir

apercevoir — to perceive
concevoir — to conceive

décevoir — to deceive

35. *RESOUDRE* [TO RESOLVE]

1	2	3	4	5
résoudre	*résolvant*	*résolu*	*je résous*	*je résolus*

| | | | PAST INDEFINITE
j'ai résolu | je résous
tu résous
il résout
nous résolvons
vous résolvez
ils résolvent | |

LIKE *Résoudre*: *dissoudre*, to dissolve (in the first, second, and fourth principal parts, but different in the third and fifth; its past participle is *dissous*, *fem. dissoute*, and it lacks the past definite and imperfect subjunctive tenses).

36. *RIRE* [TO LAUGH]

1	2	3	4	5
rire	*riant*	*ri*	*je ris*	*je ris*

| | | | PAST INDEFINITE
j'ai ri | je ris
tu ris
il rit
nous rions
vous riez
ils rient | |

LIKE *Rire*: *sourire*, to smile

37. *SAVOIR* [TO KNOW, KNOW HOW]

1	2	3	4	5
savoir	*sachant*	*su*	*je sais*	*je sus*

| FUTURE
je saurai | IMPERFECT
je savais [&c.]

PRESENT
SUBJUNCTIVE
je sache
tu saches
il sache
nous sachions
vous sachiez
ils sachent | PAST
INDEFINITE
j'ai su | je sais
tu sais
il sait
nous savons
vous savez
ils savent

IMPERATIVE
sache
sachons
sachez |

38. *SUFFIRE* [TO SUFFICE]

1 *suffire*	2 *suffisant*	3 *suffi*	4 *je suffis*	5 *je suffis*
		PAST INDEFINITE j'ai suffi	je suffis tu suffis il suffit nous suffisons vous suffisez ils suffisent	

39. *SUIVRE* [TO FOLLOW]

1 *suivre*	2 *suivant*	3 *suivi*	4 *je suis*	5 *je suivis*
		PAST INDEFINITE j'ai suivi	je suis tu suis il suit nous suivons vous suivez ils suivent	

LIKE *Suivre*: *poursuivre*, to pursue

40. *TENIR* [TO HOLD]

1 *tenir*	2 *tenant*	3 *tenu*	4 *je tiens*	5 *je tins*
FUTURE je tiendrai	PRESENT SUBJUNCTIVE je tienne tu tiennes il tienne nous tenions vous teniez ils tiennent	PAST INDEFINITE j'ai tenu	je tiens tu tiens il tient nous tenons vous tenez ils tiennent	tu tins il tint nous tînmes vous tîntes ils tinrent IMPERFECT SUBJUNCTIVE je tinsse [&c.]

LIKE *Tenir*

appartenir	to belong	*obtenir*	to obtain
contenir	to contain	*retenir*	to retain
maintenir	to maintain	*soutenir*	to sustain

Also like *tenir*: *venir* and all its compounds, except that most of them are conjugated with *être*.

venir (être)	to come	*prévenir (avoir)*	to warn
convenir (avoir)	to suit	*revenir (être)*	to come back
devenir (être)	to become	*se souvenir*	to remember
parvenir (être)	to attain		

41. *VALOIR* [TO BE WORTH]

1 *valoir*	2 *valant*	3 *valu*	4 *je vaux*	5 *je valus*
FUTURE je vaudrai	PRESENT SUBJUNCTIVE je vaille tu vailles il vaille nous valions vous valiez ils vaillent	PAST INDEFINITE j'ai valu	je vaux tu vaux il vaut nous valons vous valez ils valent	

LIKE *Valoir*: *prévaloir*, to prevail

42. *VIVRE* [TO LIVE]

1 *vivre*	2 *vivant*	3 *vécu*	4 *je vis*	5 *je vécus*
		PAST INDEFINITE j'ai vécu	je vis tu vis il vit nous vivons vous vivez ils vivent	

43. *VOIR* [TO SEE]

1 *voir*	2 *voyant*	3 *vu*	4 *je vois*	5 *je vis*
FUTURE je verrai	PRESENT SUBJUNCTIVE je voie tu voies il voie nous voyions vous voyiez ils voient	PAST INDEFINITE j'ai vu	je vois tu vois il voit nous voyons vous voyez ils voient	

LIKE *Voir*: *pourvoir*, to provide, *prévoir*, to foresee
except that the future and conditional are formed regularly from the infinitive
stem (*je pourvoirai, je prévoirai*) and the past definite of *pourvoir* is *pourvus*.

44. *VOULOIR* [to want, wish]

1 *vouloir*	2 *voulant*	3 *voulu*	4 *je veux*	5 *je voulus*
FUTURE	PRESENT SUBJUNCTIVE	PAST INDEFINITE	je veux	
je voudrai	je veuille	j'ai voulu	tu veux	
	tu veuilles		il veut	
	il veuille		nous voulons	
	nous voulions		vous voulez	
	vous vouliez		ils veulent	
	ils veuillent			

INDEX OF IRREGULAR VERBS

The numbers refer to the list of irregular verbs
in the preceding pages.

accourir, 12
accueillir, 16
acquérir, 3
admettre, 25
aller, 4
apercevoir, 34
apparaître, 10
appartenir, 40
apprendre, 33
asseoir, 5
atteindre, 13
avoir, 1

battre, 6
boire, 7
bouillir, 29

commettre, 25
comprendre, 33
concevoir, 34
conclure, 8
conduire, 9
connaître, 10
conquérir, 3
consentir, 29
construire, 9
contenir, 40
contraindre, 13
contredire, 18
convenir, 40
coudre, 11
courir, 12
couvrir, 28
craindre, 13
croire, 14
croître, 15
cueillir, 16

décevoir, 34
décrire, 19
défaire, 21
détruire, 9
devenir, 40
devoir, 17
dire, 18
dissoudre, 35
disparaître, 10

dormir, 29

écrire, 19
élire, 24
entreprendre, 33
envoyer, 20
éteindre, 13
être, 2
exclure, 8

faire, 21
falloir, 22
feindre, 13
fuir, 23

inscrire, 19
instruire, 9
introduire, 9

joindre, 13

lire, 24

maintenir, 40
médire, 18
mentir, 29
mettre, 25
mourir, 26

naître, 27

obtenir, 40
offrir, 28
ouvrir, 28

paraître, 10
parcourir, 12
partir, 29
parvenir, 40
peindre, 13
permettre, 25
plaindre, 13
plaire, 30
pleuvoir, 31
poindre, 13
poursuivre, 39
pourvoir, 43

pouvoir, 32
prédire, 18
prendre, 33
prévaloir, 41
prévenir, 40
prévoir, 43
produire, 9
promettre, 25

recevoir, 34
reconnaître, 10
réduire, 9
renaître, 27
repentir, 29
résoudre, 35
restreindre, 13
retenir, 40
revenir, 40
rire, 36

satisfaire, 21
savoir, 37
secourir, 12
sentir, 29
servir, 29
sortir, 29
souffrir, 28
soumettre, 25
sourire, 36
soutenir, 40
souvenir, 40
suffire, 38
suivre, 39
surprendre, 33

taire, 30
teindre, 13
tenir, 40
traduire, 9
tressaillir, 16

valoir, 41
venir, 40
vivre, 42
voir, 43
vouloir, 44

French–English Vocabulary

VOCABULARY required for the translation of an exercise is not always listed here if it already occurs in the text of the lesson. However, if it is needed for the exercises of *other* lessons, it does appear.

The simple elementary forms, such as articles and personal pronouns, are omitted, as are obvious cognates. Numerals are given in Appendix C.

ABBREVIATIONS

adj.	adjective	*m.*	masculine
adv.	adverb	*n.*	noun
conj.	conjunction	*p. p.*	past participle
dem.	demonstrative	*pl.*	plural
f.	feminine	*prep.*	preposition
impers.	impersonal	*pron.*	pronoun
inf.	infinitive	*v.*	verb

abord : d'abord *adv.* first; **tout d'abord** at first
aborder *v.* to take up
abrégé *m.* abridgment, summary
accompagner *v.* to accompany
accomplir *v.* to accomplish
accord *m.* agreement; **se mettre d'accord** to agree
accrocher *v.* to hang up; **s'accrocher à** to cling to
acheter *v.* to buy
achever *v.* to complete, finish
acquérir *v.* to acquire
actualité *f.* current events, current topics
actuel, actuelle *adj.* present, current; **actuellement** *adv.* at the present time, currently
affirmer *v.* to assert, declare, state

agence *f.* agency; **agence de placement** employment agency
agent *m.* **agent de police** policeman
agir *v.* to act; **il s'agit de** (*impers.*) it is a question of
aider *v.* to help
ailleurs *adv.* elsewhere; **d'ailleurs** moreover
aimantation *f.* magnetization
aimer *v.* to like, love
ainsi *adv.* thus; **ainsi que** as well as
ajouter *v.* to add
alimentation *f.* food, food supply
allée *f.* lane, path, walk
alléger *v.* to lighten
aller *v.* to go; **s'en aller** to go away, leave

alors *adv.* then; **alors que** *conj.* whereas, while

amélioration *f.* improvement, amelioration

aménager *v.* to lay out, set up

amener *v.* to bring

américain, américaine *adj.* American

ami *m.* **amie** *f.* friend

amical, amicale *adj.* friendly, amicable

amplificateur, amplificatrice *n.* amplifier

amuser *v.* to amuse, entertain; **s'amuser** to have a good time

an *m.* year

ancien, ancienne *adj.* old, ancient; former (*see* Lesson VIII, paragraph 4c)

anglais, anglaise *adj.* English; **anglais** *n. m.* English (language)

Angleterre *f.* England

année *f.* year

août *m.* August

apercevoir *v.* **s'apercevoir de** to perceive

aperçu *m.* rapid survey

apparaître *v.* to appear

appareil *m.* apparatus, device, appliance

apparence *f.* appearance

appartenir *v.* to belong

appeler *v.* to call; **s'appeler** to be called, to be named; **Comment s'appelle-t-il?** What is his name?

appliquer *v.* to apply

apporter *v.* to bring

apprécier *v.* to appreciate; to appraise

apprendre *v.* to learn

approfondi, approfondie (*p. p.* of **approfondir** used as *adj.*) thorough

approfondir *v.* to investigate, examine thoroughly

approuver *v.* to approve

appuyé, appuyée (*p. p.* of **appuyer**) *adj.* supported (by), leaning (upon)

après *prep.* after; *adv.* afterward, next

après-midi *m.* afternoon

arabe *adj.* Arabic, Arab; *n. m.* Arabic (language)

arbre *m.* tree

arbuste *f.* bush, shrub

argent *m.* money

armée *f.* army

arriver *v.* to arrive, come; to happen; **arriver à** (+ *inf.*) to succeed

aspect *m.* aspect, appearance

asseoir *r.* to seat; **s'asseoir** to sit down

assez *adv.* enough; rather

assister *v.* **assister à** to attend, be present at

astronome *m.* astronomer (*see* Lesson XIV, paragraph 3)

attendre *v.* to wait, wait for; **s'attendre à** to expect

attendrir *v.* **s'attendrir** to be moved, grow emotional

attentivement *adv.* attentively

aucun, aucune *adj.* no, not any

au-dessus de *prep.* above, over

augmenter *v.* to augment, increase; **augmenter quelqu'un** to give someone a raise in pay

aujourd'hui *adv.* today

auprès de *prep.* near; among (*see* Appendix A)

aussi *adv.* also; therefore, so (when first in sentence); **aussi ... que** as ... as

auteur *m.* author

auto-critique *f.* self-criticism

automne *m.* autumn

autour de *prep.* around

autre *adj.* other, different; **l'un(e) l'autre, les uns les autres** each other, one another (*see* Lesson IV, paragraph 2)

autrefois *adv.* formerly

autrement *adv.* otherwise

avant (de) *prep.* before; **avant que** *conj.* before; **en avant** *adv.* forward; **avant tout** especially

avantage *m.* advantage

avec *prep.* with; **d'avec** from

avenir *m.* future

avertir *v.* to notify

aviateur *m.* aviator

avion *m.* airplane

avis *m.* opinion

avocat *m.* lawyer

avoir *v.* to have (auxiliary for past tenses); **il y a** there is, there are; **il y a ... que, il y avait ... que** (for use with expressions of time and present and imperfect tenses, *see* Lesson III, paragraph 1); **il y a** (+ expression of time) ago (*see* Lesson III, Idioms)

barrière *f.* gate

bateau *m.* (*pl.* **bateaux**) boat

bâtir *v.* to build

battre *v.* to strike, beat; **se battre** to fight

bavarder *v.* to talk, gossip

beau (**bel, belle, beaux, belles**) *adj.* beautiful, fine

beaucoup *adv.* much, greatly, a lot; **beaucoup de** much, many, a lot of

Belgique *f.* Belgium

belliqueux, belliqueuse *adj.* bellicose

bénéficier *v.* to benefit, profit

besoin *m.* need; **avoir besoin de** to need

bête *f.* animal, creature

bêtise *f.* stupidity, silly thing

bibliothèque *f.* library

bicyclette *f.* bicycle

bientôt *adv.* soon

bienveillant *adj.* benevolent

bilan *m.* balance sheet; report

bizarre *adj.* bizarre, peculiar

blanc, blanche *adj.* white

blesser *v.* to wound, injure, hurt

bœuf *m.* beef

boire *v.* to drink

bois *m.* wood

bord *m.* **à bord de** *prep.* aboard

botanique *f.* botany

bouder *v.* to sulk, pout

bouillir *v.* to boil

bout *m.* end; **au bout de** at the end of, after

brave *adj.* brave; fine (*see* Lesson VIII, paragraph 4c)

bref, brève *adj.* brief

brillant, brillante *adj.* brilliant

brique *f.* brick

bruit *m.* noise, sound

bruyant, bruyante *adj.* noisy

bureau *m.* (*pl.* **bureaux**) desk; office; **bureau de poste** post office

but *m.* goal, aim

cacher *v.* to hide

cadeau *m.* gift

cale *f.* wedge

camarade *m.* comrade, chum, mate; **camarade de chambre** roommate

campagne *f.* country

canne *f.* cane

capital, capitale *adj.* capital, principal; *n. m.* (often *pl.* **capitaux**) capital (in financial sense)

car *conj.* for, because

caractère *m.* character; disposition; temper

caractériser *v.* to characterize

carte *f.* card; map

cartographie *f.* cartography

cas *m.* case

cause *f.* cause; **en cause** in question

causer *v.* to chat, talk

céder *v.* to yield, give up

ce, cet, cette *dem. adj.* this, that; (*pl.*) **ces** these, those; **ce** *dem. pron.* it, he, she, that, this, these, those, they; **ce qui, ce que** what, that which, which (*see* Lessons X, paragraph 1 and 2b, and XI, paragraph 1c)

cela *dem. pron.* that, it (*see* Lesson X, paragraph 2b)

célèbre *adj.* famous

centaine *f.* a hundred, a hundred or so (*see* Appendix C)

certes *adv.* certainly

cesser *v.* to cease, stop

chaleur *f.* heat

chanter *v.* to sing

chapeau *m.* hat

chaque *adj.* each, every; **chaque fois que** whenever

charger *v.* to load

chat *m.* cat

chaux *f.* lime

chef *m.* chief

chemin *m.* road; **chemin de fer** railroad

cher, chère *adj.* dear; **cher** *adv.* dearly, expensively

chercher *v.* to look for, seek

cherté *f.* high cost

chez *prep.* at the home of, to the home of; at (to) the office of; in the works of; in, among; **chez moi** at my home, at home, to my home, home, back home, in my country

chiffre *m.* figure

chimie *f.* chemistry

chimique *adj.* chemical

chlorhydrique *adj.* hydrochloric

chlorure *m.* chloride

choisir *v.* to choose

choix *m.* choice

chômage *m.* unemployment

chose *f.* thing

chute *f.* fall

ciel *m.* (*pl.* **cieux**) sky

clair, claire *adj.* clear

clouer *v.* to nail

coin *m.* corner

collègue *m.* colleague

colline *f.* hill

combien (**de**) *adv.* how much, how many

combiner *v.* **se combiner** to combine

combustible *m.* fuel; *adj.* combustible

comédienne *f.* actress, comedienne

comme *conj.* like, as; as if; as it were; **comme d'habitude** as usual

comment *adv.* how

commettre *v.* to commit

commode *adj.* convenient

commun, commune *adj.* common; **la mise en commun** pooling

communauté *f.* community

compagnon *m.* companion; mate

complaisant, complaisante *adj.* complacent

compliqué, compliquée *adj.* complex, complicated

comporter *v.* to involve

composé *m.* compound (*see* **corps composé**)

comprendre *v.* to understand

compte *m.* account; **se rendre compte de** to realize; **faire ses comptes** to add up one's accounts, balance one's books.

compter *v.* to count; intend, expect

compte-rendu *m.* report

concerner *v.* to concern; **en ce qui concerne** as regards, as concerns

concurrent *m.* competitor

conduire *v.* to lead, conduct; to drive (an automobile)

conférence *f.* lecture; conference

connaissance *f.* knowledge

connaître *v.* to know, be acquainted with; to become acquainted with; se connaître en, s'y connaître en to know all about, to be a good judge of; s'y connaître to know all about it (them), be a good judge of it (them) (*see* Lesson II, paragraphs 5 and 8)

connu, connue (*p. p.* of connaître) *adj.* well known

conscient, consciente *adj.* conscious

conseiller *m.* adviser

constater *v.* to observe, state; to establish, ascertain

constituant *m.* constituent

constituer *v.* to constitute, make up

construire *v.* to construct

contenir *v.* to contain

contenu *m.* content

convaincre *v.* to convince

corde *f.* rope, cord

coréen, coréenne *adj.* Korean

corps *m.* body; corps composé compound

corriger *v.* to correct

costume *m.* suit

côté *m.* side; direction; de ce côté on this (that) side, in this (that) direction; de tous côtés on all sides; de l'autre côté on the other side; de mon côté for my part; à côté de beside; à côté next door; du côté de in the direction of, toward

coup *m.* blow, blast

couper *v.* to cut

courant *m.* current; au courant de informed of; se tenir au courant to keep informed; courant, courante *adj.* current; running, fluent

courir *v.* to run

couramment *adv.* fluently

cours *m.* course; au cours de in the course of

coûter *v.* to cost; coûter cher to cost a lot

coutume *f.* custom

couturière *f.* dressmaker, seamstress

couvrir *v.* to cover; se couvrir to be covered, become covered; (of the sky) to become cloudy

craindre *v.* to fear

crainte *f.* fear; de crainte que for fear that

cratère *m.* crater

créer *v.* to create

critique *f.* criticism; *m.* critic, *adj.* critical (*see* Lesson VIII, paragraph 4d)

critiquer *v.* to criticize

croire *v.* to believe, think

croître *v.* to grow

cuisine *f.* kitchen; cooking, cuisine

cultiver *v.* to cultivate, raise

curé *m.* priest (pastor of a parish)

dans *prep.* in, into, within, etc.

danse *f.* dance

davantage *adv.* more

de *prep.* of; from; (as partitive article) some, any (*see* Lesson XIV)

débarrasser *v.* se débarrasser de to get rid of

décourager *v.* to discourage

découvert (*p. p.* of découvrir, to discover)

découverte *f.* discovery

défaut *m.* defect

défendre *v.* to defend; to forbid

défunt, défunte *adj.* deceased

dégager *v.* to release, liberate, set free

dehors *adv.* outside; en dehors de *prep.* outside, beyond

déjà *adv.* already

déjeuner *v.* to lunch, to eat lunch

demain *adv.* tomorrow

demander *v.* to ask, ask for, require; **se demander** to wonder

demi, demie *adj.* half

démission *f.* resignation

dépasser *v.* to exceed, surpass

depuis *prep.* since, for (*see* Lesson III); **depuis quand** how long; **depuis ... jusqu'à** from ... to

déranger *v.* to disturb

dernier, dernière *adj.* last

dès *prep.* from, as early as

désagréable *adj.* disagreeable

désagréger *v.* to break up, separate

descendre *v.* to go down, descend; to take down (*see* Lesson I, paragraph 7)

désormais *adv.* henceforth

détruire *v.* to destroy

développer *v.* to develop; **se développer** to develop

devenir *v.* to become; **Qu'est-ce qu'il est devenu?** What has become of him?

deviner *v.* to guess

devoir *v.* (with *n.* or *pron.* object) to owe; (followed by an *inf.*) must, have to, ought, etc. (*see* Lesson V); **devoir** *m.* duty; *m. pl.* exercises, homework

diagnostic *m.* diagnosis

différer *v.* to defer, postpone; to differ

difficile *adj.* difficult

dire *v.* to say, tell; **dire que...** to think that ... (*see* Lesson VI, paragraph 13)

disposer *v.* to arrange; **disposer de** to have available, to have at one's disposal

disposition *f.* disposal; arrangement

distrait, distraite *adj.* distracted, absent-minded

divaguer *v.* to digress, ramble, wander incoherently from the subject

divers, diverse *adj.* diverse

diviser *v.* to divide

dix ten

dizaine *f.* about ten

domaine *m.* field, domain

donc *adv.* therefore, so; (or to show emphasis)

donnée *f.* **les données** data

donner *v.* to give

dormir *v.* to sleep

doute *m.* **sans doute** no doubt, probably

douter (de) *v.* to doubt

doux, douce *adj.* sweet, gentle; soft

dresser *v.* to draw up

droit, droite *adj.* straight; **droit** *adv.* straight

dur, dure *adj.* hard

durée *f.* duration, continuance

eau *f.* water; **eau potable** drinking water

ébullition *f.* boiling, boiling point

école *f.* school

échantillon *m.* sample

économiser *v.* to save

écouter *v.* to listen (to)

écrire *v.* to write

écriteau *m.* sign, notice

écrivain *m.* writer

effectuer *v.* to carry out, accomplish

effet *m.* effect; **en effet** in fact

efforcer *v.* **s'efforcer (de)** to make an effort, endeavor

égarer *v.* **s'égarer** to get lost

électrolysable *adj.* capable of undergoing electrolysis

électrolyse *f.* electrolysis

élève *m.* or *f.* pupil, student

élever *v.* to raise; **s'élever** to rise, get up

emballage *m.* packing
émerveiller *v.* to amaze
emmener *v.* to take (a person away somewhere)
émolument *m. (pl.)* wages
employer *v.* to use
emporter *v.* to take away, carry away (a thing); **l'emporter** to win (a victory)
en *prep.* in, into, to; while, by, in, on (or untranslatable) when used with present participle (*see* Lesson III, paragraphs 2 and 7; Lesson IX, paragraph 2d)
encore *adv.* still, yet; again; **pas encore** not yet
encre *f.* ink
endroit *m.* place
enfance *f.* childhood
enfant *m.* or *f.* child
enfermer *v.* to lock up, lock in, shut up
enfin *adv.* finally
énormément *adv.* enormously
enregistrement *m.* recording
enregistrer *v.* to record, register
enseignement *m.* teaching, education
ensemble *adv.* together; *n. m.* whole; group; over-all organization
ensuivre *v.* **il s'ensuit que** it follows that
entendre *v.* to hear
enterrement *m.* burial
enthousiasme *m.* enthusiasm
entourer *v.* to surround, encircle
entraîner *v.* to carry away, sweep away; to involve; to train
entreprendre *v.* to undertake
entrer *v.* to go in, come in, enter; **entrer dans** to enter (+ direct object)
entretenir *v.* to maintain; to converse with, entertain
envie *f.* envy; desire

environ *adv.* about, approximately; **environs** *m. pl.* neighborhood, vicinity
envoyer *v.* to send; **envoyer chercher** to send for
épais, épaisse *adj.* thick
épaisseur *f.* thickness
époque *f.* time, period
épouse *f.* wife, spouse
éprouver *v.* to test, try; to experience
éprouvette *f.* test tube
ère *f.* era
erreur *f.* error, mistake
espèce *f.* kind
espérer *v.* to hope
esprit *m.* mind, intelligence; spirit; wit
essayer *v.* to try
essor *m.* soaring, impetus, impulse
essuyer *v.* to wipe
estival, estivale *adj.* referring to summer, summer
étage *m.* floor; **premier étage** second floor
état *m.* state, condition
Etats-Unis *m. pl.* United States
été *m.* summer
éteindre *v.* to extinguish, put out
étendre *v.* to extend; **s'étendre** to extend, to be extended
étonnant, étonnante *adj.* astonishing
étonner *v.* to astonish, startle, surprise
étrange *adj.* strange
étranger, étrangère *adj.* foreign; **étranger** *m.* foreigner; **étrangère** *f.* foreigner; **à l'étranger** abroad, in foreign countries
étroitement *adv.* closely, tightly
étude *f.* study
étudiant *m.* student
étudier *v.* to study
européen, européenne *adj.* European

évanouir: s'évanouir v. to faint
éveillé, éveillée adj. awake; wide awake, sharp
éveiller v. to awaken
événement m. event
évidemment adv. obviously, of course
éviter v. to avoid (see Lesson VI, paragraph 10)
exemple m. example
exiger v. to demand
expédier v. to dispatch
expérience f. experiment; experience
expérimenter v. to experiment with, to test
explication f. explanation
expliquer v. to explain
exposé m. explanation, account
exposer v. to set forth, expound, explain
exprimer v. to express

fâcheux, fâcheuse adj. troublesome, unfortunate
façon f. manner
faible adj. weak; low, small
faire v. to make, to do; (followed by inf.) to make, cause, have, get; se faire to be done; to become; to form; se faire à to get accustomed to; faire mal à to hurt; se faire attendre to be long in coming; faire le sourd to pretend to be deaf; il fait beau it is nice weather; faire du bien à to do good to; qu'est-ce que cela leur fait what difference does that make to them; faire partie de to belong to (see Lesson VII)
fait m. fact; de fait in fact
falloir impers. v. to be necessary, must, to be needed (see Lesson V, paragraph 6); il s'en faut de peu very nearly (see Lesson V, paragraph 7b)

famille f. family
fantôme m. ghost
faute f. mistake, error
faux, fausse adj. false
feindre v. to feign, pretend
féliciter v. to congratulate
femelle f. female
femme f. woman; femme de ménage cleaning woman
ferroviaire adj. pertaining to railways; le réseau ferroviaire the railway system
feu m. fire
fille f. daughter; petite fille little girl; jeune fille girl, young lady
fin f. end
finir v. to finish
fixer v. to fix, settle, determine
flacon m. flask, bottle
fleur f. flower
fleuve m. river
fois f. time; une fois once; deux fois twice
fonction f. function, position, office
fonctionner v. to function
fond m. bottom; à fond thoroughly
fonder v. to found
force f. (often in plural) strength, force; à force de by dint of
former v. to form, train
fort, forte adj. strong; fort n. m. fort; fort adv. very, quite; loudly
fou (fol, folle, fous, folles) adj. crazy
fournir v. to furnish, supply
frais m. pl. expense; à ses frais at his own expense
frais, fraîche adj. fresh, cool
français, française adj. French; français n. m. French (language); Français m. Frenchman
franciser v. to gallicize, to Frenchify
frapper v. to strike

frère *m.* brother
froisser *v.* to offend
fumée *f.* smoke
furieusement *adv.* furiously

gages *m. pl.* wages
galant, galante *adj.* gallant
gant *m.* glove
garçon *m.* boy
garder *v.* to keep
geler *v.* to freeze
gêné, gênée *adj.* uneasy, embarrassed, troubled
génie *m.* genius; engineering
gens *m. pl.* people
gentil, gentille *adj.* nice, amiable
goûter *v.* to taste; to appreciate, relish
gracieux, gracieuse *adj.* graceful; gracious
grammaire *f.* grammar
grand, grande *adj.* large; tall; great
grand'chose *pron. m.* **pas grand'-chose** not much
grandir *v.* to grow
grand-mère *f.* grandmother
grand-père *m.* grandfather
gré *m.* liking, will, taste
grenouille *f.* frog
gronder *v.* to scold
guérir *v.* to cure
guerre *f.* war

('h = aspirate *h*)
habile *adj.* able, clever
habiter *v.* to live (in), dwell (in)
habitude *f.* habit; **comme d'habitude** as usual
hardi, hardie *adj.* bold
hausse *f.* rise, advance
herbe *f.* grass
hériter (de) *v.* to inherit
héros *m.* hero
heure *f.* hour, time; **deux heures** two o'clock; **deux heures et demie** two-thirty

heureux, heureuse *adj.* happy
hier *adv.* yesterday
histoire *f.* history; story
homme *m.* man
houille *f.* coal
huile *f.* oil
hydrate *m.* hydrate, hydroxide
hypothèse *f.* hypothesis

ici *adv.* here; **par ici** hereabouts, around here; this way
idée *f.* idea
illustre *adj.* famous, illustrious
immeuble *m.* building
impôt *m.* tax
impressionnant, impressionnante *adj.* impressive
imprimer *v.* to imprint, impress
inachevé, inachevée *adj.* incomplete
inaugurer *v.* to inaugurate, open
infirme *adj.* disabled, crippled; feeble
ingénieur *m.* engineer; **ingénieur en chef** chief engineer
initiateur *m.* initiator
inoculer *v.* to inoculate
inspecteur *m.* inspector
installer *v.* **s'installer** to move in, settle down
instruire *v.* to instruct, educate
instruit, instruite *adj.* educated, well-educated
intéressant, intéressante *adj.* interesting
intéressé, intéressée *adj.* biased, self-interested, interested
intéresser *v.* **s'intéresser à** to take an interest in, to be interested in
intérêt *m.* interest, self-interest
intime *adj.* intimate
introduire *v.* to introduce
invité *m.* guest
issue *f.* way out, solution; **à l'issue de** on the way out from

jamais *adv.* ever; never; **ne ... jamais** *adv.* (*see* Lesson VI, paragraph 7a) never

jardinier *m.* gardener

jeter *v.* to throw, cast

jeune *adj.* young; **jeune fille** girl

jeunesse *f.* youth

joli, jolie *adj.* pretty

jouer *v.* to play

jouet *m.* toy, plaything

jouir (de) *v.* to enjoy

jour *m.* day

juge *m.* judge

juger *v.* to judge, deem

juin *m.* June

jusque: **jusqu'à** *prep.* even to, as far as

juste *adv.* just, exactly

justifier *v.* to justify; **se justifier** to be justified

klaxon *m.* horn

là *adv.* there; **par là** that way; **c'est par là que** that is where

laborieux, laborieuse *adj.* laborious

laisser *v.* to leave

lait *m.* milk

langue *f.* language

large *adj.* broad; **largement** *adv.* largely, broadly, amply

leçon *f.* lesson

lecture *f.* reading

léger, légère *adj.* light

légitime *adj.* legitimate

lentement *adv.* slowly

lettre *f.* letter

lever *v.* **se lever** to get up, rise

libérer *v.* to liberate

librement *adv.* freely

ligne *f.* line

lire *v.* to read

littéraire *adj.* literary

livre *m.* book

livrer *v.* to deliver, hand over; **se livrer** to give in; to confide

logiquement *adv.* logically

long, longue *adj.* long; **le long de** along

longtemps *adv.* long, a long time

lors de *prep.* at the time of

lorsque *conj.* when

louer *v.* to praise

loupe *f.* magnifying glass

lourdement *adv.* heavily

lumière *f.* light

lunaire *adj.* lunar

lune *f.* moon

machine *f.*: **machine à écrire** typewriter

maintenant *adv.* now

maintenir *v.* to maintain

mais *conj.* but

maison *f.* house, home; building, apartment building

maisonette *f.* small house, cottage

maître *m.* master, teacher

maîtriser *v.* to control

mal *m.* harm, trouble; *adv.* poorly, badly; **faire mal à** to hurt

malade *adj.* sick, ill

malgré *prep.* in spite of

manger *v.* to eat

manière *f.* manner, way; **de cette manière** in this way

mannequin *m.* mannequin, fashion model

manquer *v.* to fail; to miss; to lack; **manquer à** to be lacking to

marche *f.* movement, progress, advance

marcher *v.* to walk; to march; to go, run

mari *m.* husband

marié, mariée (*p.p.* of **marier**) *adj.* married

marier *v.* to marry, marry off (as applied to the clergyman or the parents of the couple concerned); **se marier** to get married

marin, marine *adj.* marine
marquer *v.* to mark
matériaux *n. m. pl.* materiels
matériel *m.* materiel, equipment
matière *f.* matter
matin *m.* morning
mécanique *f.* mechanics; *adj.* mechanical
méchant, méchante *adj.* wicked; naughty
médecin *m.* physician, doctor
meilleur, meilleure *adj.* better (*see* Lesson VIII, paragraph 6)
mélange *m.* mixture
même *adj.* same; self, very; *adv.* even (*see* Lesson VIII, paragraph 4c)
mener *v.* to lead, take, bring
mentir *v.* to lie
mère *f.* mother
merveilleux, merveilleuse *adj.* marvelous
métal *m.* (*pl.* **métaux**) metal
mètre *m.* meter
mettre *v.* to place, put, set; **mettre en accusation** to accuse, indict, arraign; **mettre en valeur** develop; etc. (*see* Lesson III, Idioms); **se mettre à** to begin
meuble *m.* piece of furniture; **meubles** *pl.* furniture
mieux *adv.* (comparative of **bien**) better; best
milieu *m.* middle, midst; **au milieu de** in the midst of, among
millier *m.* about a thousand (*see* Appendix C)
minéral *m.* (*pl.* **minéraux**) mineral
minuit *m.* midnight
mis (*p. p.* of **mettre**): **mis à part** apart from
mise *f.* putting, placing (*see* **mettre**); **la mise en commun** pooling; **la mise en liberté** freeing, etc.; **la mise sur orbite** orbiting, putting in orbit

mode *f.* style; **à la mode** in fashion
moins *adv.* less; **à moins que** unless
mois *m.* month
monde *m.* world; society; people
mondial, mondiale *adj.* worldwide
monsieur *m.* sir; mister; gentleman
montagne *f.* mountain
monter *v.* (conjugated with **être**) to go up, climb up, mount, ascend; (conjugated with **avoir**) to take up, carry up, to go up(stairs)
montre *f.* watch
montrer *v.* to show
mot *m.* word
mou (**mol, molle, mous, molles**) *adj.* soft
mourir *v.* (conjugated with **être**) to die
mouvoir *v.* **se mouvoir** to move
moyen *m.* means
muet, muette *adj.* mute, dumb
mur *m.* wall; **passage du mur du son** breaking the sound barrier

nage *f.* swimming; **traverser à la nage** swim across
naissance *f.* birth
naître *v.* (conjugated with **être**) to be born
natal, natale *adj.* native
ne *adv.* the first part of all French negatives when they are used with a verb; sometimes stands as a complete negative in the meaning "not"; sometimes pleonastic (*see* Lesson VI for complete treatment)
ni *adv.* nor; **ni ... ni** neither ... nor
nid *m.* nest
niveau (*pl.* **niveaux**) *m.* level
nom *m.* name; **de nom** in name

nombre *m.* number
nombreux, nombreuse *adj.* numerous
nouveau (nouvel, nouvelle, nouveaux, nouvelles) *adj.* new
nouvelle *f.* piece of news, news
noyau *m.* nucleus
nu, nue *adj.* naked
nul, nulle *adj.* no; **nulle part** nowhere

objet *m.* object
obtenir *v.* to obtain
occasion *f.* occasion, chance
occuper *v.* **s'occuper de** to concern oneself with, busy oneself with
œil (*pl.* **yeux**) *m.* eye
œuvre *f.* work (literary, charitable, etc.)
officier *m.* officer
offrir *v.* to offer
oiseau (*pl.* **oiseaux**) bird
omettre *v.* omit
on *pron.* one, we, you, they, people, someone (*see* Lesson III, paragraph 5)
oncle *m.* uncle
opérer *v.* to operate, effect
organiser *v.* to organize
où *conj.* where, in which; when
oublier *v.* to forget
ouvert, ouverte (*p.p.* of **ouvrir**) *adj.* open
ouvrage *m.* work
ouvrier *m.* workman
ouvrir *v.* to open

pâle *adj.* pale
papier *m.* paper
paquet *m.* package
par *prep.* by; through; **par ici** hereabouts, around here; this way
paradoxalement *adv.* paradoxically
paraître *v.* to appear; to be published

parce que *conj.* because
parcourir *v.* to run through, cover, go all over
parfaitement *adv.* perfectly
parfois *adv.* sometimes
parler *v.* to speak
parole *f.* word; **prendre la parole** (*see* **prendre**)
part *f.* share, portion; **quelque part** somewhere; **d'une part** ... **d'autre part** on the one hand ... on the other hand; **de part et d'autre** on both sides; **à part** aside; **mis à part** apart from
participer *v.* **participer à** to participate in
particularité *f.* peculiarity, individual characteristic
particule *f.* particle
particulier, particulière *adj.* private; special
partie *f.* part (*see* Lesson XII, Idioms, and Lesson XIV, paragraph 3)
partir *v.* (conjugated with **être**) to go away, leave, depart, set out
pas: ne ... pas *adv.* not; *n. m.* pace, step
passage *m.* **passage à niveau** grade crossing
passager *m.* passenger
passé, passée (*p.p.* of **passer**) *adj.* past, last; **passé** *n. m.* past
passer *v.* to spend; **se passer** to take place; **se passer de** to do without; **passer l'été à entraîner** to spend the summer training
patron *m.* employer; proprietor; boss
pays *m.* country
peinture *f.* painting
pendant *prep.* during; **pendant que** *conj.* while
penser *v.* to think; **penser à** to think about
perdre *v.* to lose

père *m.* father
perfectionnement *m.* improvement, perfecting
perfectionner *v.* to improve, perfect; **se perfectionner** to improve, to be improved, to be perfected
permanent, permanente *adj.* permanent
permettre *v.* to permit
personne *n. f.* person; *pron. m.* nobody (*see* Lesson VI, paragraph 7c)
pesant, pesante *adj.* heavy
peser *v.* to weigh
petit, petite *adj.* little, small
peu *adv.* little, few; not, un-, in-, etc.; **un peu** somewhat; **peu de chose** very unimportant, a mere trifle
peur *f.* fear; **avoir peur de (que)** to fear; **de peur que** for fear that
peut-être *adv.* perhaps, maybe
phénomène *m.* phenomenon; **phénomènes** phenomena
photographie *f.* photograph (*see* Lesson XIV, paragraph 3)
physique *f.* physics; *adj.* physical
pièce *f.* piece; apiece; play, drama; room
pied *m.* foot; **à pied** on foot
pierre *f.* stone
pitié *f.* pity
place *f.* city square, plaza; seat; place; room (space)
placement: **agence de placement** employment agency
placer *v.* to place, put
plaindre *v.* to pity; **se plaindre de** to complain of
plaire *v.* to please; **cela me plaît** I like that; **s'il vous plaît** please, if you please
plan *m.* plan; plane
plat *m.* dish

pleurer *v.* to weep, cry
pleuvoir *impers. v.* to rain
plupart: **la plupart des** most of, the majority of
plus *adv.* more; **le plus** the most; used as a sign of the comparative: **plus grand** taller; **plus tard** later; **ne ... plus** no longer, no more; **ne ... plus que** no longer, anything but; **non plus** either; **plus de...** no more...; **de plus en plus** more and more; **le plus** the most (*see* Lesson VI)
plusieurs *adj.* several
plutôt *adv.* rather
pneumonie *f.* pneumonia
poche *f.* pocket
poli, polie *adj.* polite
policier, policière *adj.* pertaining to the police; **roman policier** detective story
politique *adj.* political; *n. f.* politics; policy
pont *m.* bridge
porc *m.* pork
porte *f.* door; gate
portée *f.* reach, range, capacity
porter *v.* to carry, bear, bring; to wear
poste *m.* position, job
poste *f.* **bureau de poste** post office
potable *adj* drinkable; **eau potable** drinking water
potentiel, potentielle *adj.* potential; **potentiel** *n. m.* potential
poulet *m.* chicken
pour *prep.* for; (+ *inf.*) in order to; **pour que** in order that, so that
pourboire *m.* tip
pourquoi *adv.* and *conj.* why
pourtant *adv.* however, yet
pousser *v.* to push; to grow
pouvoir *v.* to be able, can, may, might; to succeed in, manage (in certain past tenses); (*see* Lesson II,

particularly paragraph 5, and Idioms)

pratique *adj.* practical; *n. f.* practice

précédent, précédente *adj.* preceding, previous

préciser *v.* to state precisely, to specify

prédécesseur *m.* predecessor

premier, première *adj.* first; **premier étage** second floor (the "first floor" in France is the first one above ground level)

prendre *v.* to take, get; **prendre la parole** to speak, take one's turn to speak

près: près de *prep.* near

pression *f.* pressure

prêter *v.* to lend

prétexter *v.* to allege (as a pretext), pretend

principal *adj.* (*m. pl.* **principaux**) principal

principe *m.* principle

printemps *m.* spring

prisonnier *m.* prisoner

prix *m.* price; prize

produire *v.* to produce; **se produire** to occur, happen

produit *m.* product

profil *m.* outline, level

projet *m.* project, plan

promener *v.* **se promener** to take a walk

prononcer *v.* **se prononcer** to declare oneself, to express one's opinion

propos *m.* remark; **tenir des propos** to make remarks

propriétaire *m.* landowner

provisoirement *adv.* provisionally, temporarily

public, publique *adj.* public; **public** *n. m.* audience, public

publier *v.* to publish

puis *adv.* then

puiser *v.* to draw; **puiser dans** to draw from

puisque *conj.* since

puissant, puissante *adj.* powerful

punir *v.* punish

quand *adv.* and *conj.* when

quant à *prep.* as for

que *pron.* whom, which, that; **que, qu'est-ce que** what; *conj.* that, as, than (*see* Lesson XIV, paragraph 1)

quelque *adj.* some; **quelques** a few; **quelque** *adv.* however; **quelques-uns, quelques-unes** *pron.* some (*see* Lesson XIII, paragraph 3c(5)(a))

qui relative *pron.* who, which, that; interrogative *pron.* who, whom

quitter *v.* to leave, abandon, quit

quoi interrogative *pron.* what

quoique *conj.* although

raconter *v.* to relate

raison *f.* reason; **avoir raison** to be right

raisonnable *adj.* rational, sensible

ramener *v.* to take back, reduce

ranger *v.* **se ranger** to line up

rapidement *adv.* rapidly, fast

rappeler *v.* to recall; **se rappeler** to remember

rapport *m.* relation, reference; report; **par rapport à** in relation, reference, proportion to

rapporter *v.* to bring back; **se rapporter** to relate, have reference to

rassurer *v.* to reassure

réaliser *v.* to achieve, accomplish, realize

récemment *adv.* recently

recevoir *v.* to receive, entertain

recherche *f.* search; inquiry; piece of research; research; **recherches** research

recommencer *v.* to begin again
recours *m.* recourse
recouvrir *v.* to cover
rédacteur *m.* editor
réduire *v.* to reduce
réflexion *f.* reflection
regarder *v.* to look at
régir *v.* to rule
règle *f.* rule, ruler
régulièrement *adv.* regularly
religieux, religieuse *adj.* religious; **religieuse** *n. f.* nun, religious
remarquer *v.* to notice
remédier (à) *v.* to remedy
remettre *v.* to deliver, hand over
remise *f.* putting back; **remise en état** reestablishment, reconstruction, restoration
remonter *v.* to go back, date back
rencontrer *v.* to meet, encounter
rendement *m.* efficiency
rendre *v.* to give back; to render, make; **se rendre** to go; surrender; **se rendre compte de (que)** to realize
renfermer *v.* to confine, contain
renseignement *m.* (piece of) information; *pl.* information
rentrer *v.* to re-enter, to return (home)
renvoyer *v.* to send back
répandre *v.* to scatter, spread; **se répandre** to spread, be diffused
repas *m.* meal
repère *m.* landmark, point of reference
répondre *v.* to answer, reply
repos *m.* rest, repose
reproduire *v.* to reproduce
réseau *m.* net; network; system
résolution *f.* **prendre une résolution** to make a resolution
résoudre *v.* to resolve, solve; **se résoudre** to be resolved, to be solved

ressembler (à) *v.* to resemble
ressource *f.* resource
rester *v.* (conjugated with **être**) to remain
restreindre *v.* to limit, restrain
restreint (*p. p.* of **restreindre**)
résultat *m.* result
retenir *v.* to retain
retirer *v.* to obtain, withdraw
retourner *v.* (conjugated with **être**) to return, go back; (with **avoir**) to turn over, around; **se retourner** to turn around
retrouver *v.* to find again, find
réunion *f.* meeting; party
réussir (à) *v.* to succeed
réussite *f.* success
révéler *v.* to reveal
revenir *v.* (conjugated with **être**) to return, come back
revenu *m.* income
revoir *v.* to see again
revue *f.* magazine, review
rien *pron.* nothing; **rien que** merely
rigoureusement *adv.* rigorously, strictly
rire *v.* to laugh
rivière *f.* river
robe *f.* dress
roche *f.* rock
roi *m.* king
roman *m.* novel; **roman policier** detective story
roucoulement *m.* cooing
rue *f.* street; **une maison rue Lamartine** a house on Lamartine street
russe *adj.* Russian; *n. m.* Russian language

sa *possessive adj.* (*see* **son**)
sage *adj.* wise; obedient, well-behaved, good
saison *f.* season
salle *f.* room; **salle de bain** bathroom

sans *prep.* without; **sans que** *conj.* without (*see* Lesson XIII, paragraph 3c (3))

satisfaisant, satisfaisante *adj.* satisfying

satisfait, satisfaite *adj.* satisfied

sauver *v.* to save; **se sauver** to run away, escape

savant *m.* scholar; scientist; **savant, savante** *adj.* learned

savoir *v.* to know; to know how to (+*inf.*); to learn, find out; to manage to, succeed in (*see* Lesson II, paragraph 5, and Idioms)

savon *m.* soap

sec, sèche *adj.* dry

secteur *m.* sector

secours *m.* help, aid

seigneur *m.* lord

sel *m.* salt; **sel de cuisine** table salt

sélénographie *f.* selenography, lunar geography

selle *f.* saddle (applied as in English to various things resembling a saddle in shape or purpose)

semaine *f.* week

sembler *v.* to seem

sensible *adj.* perceptible

sentir *v.* to feel (with the sense of touch); **se sentir** to feel (sad, sick, etc.)

serviette *f.* napkin

servir *v.* to serve; **servir de** to serve as; **se servir de** to use

ses *possessive adj.* (*see* **son**)

seul, seule *adj.* alone

seulement *adv.* only

si *conj.* if; whether; *adv.* so; yes (in answer to a negative question)

siècle *m.* century

sien: le sien, la sienne, les siens, les siennes *possessive pron.* his, hers

signalisation *f.* signaling system

simplement *adv.* simply

situer *v.* to situate

sœur *f.* sister

soigner *v.* to take care of

soir *m.* evening

sol *m.* soil, earth, ground

soldat *m.* soldier

solidaire (de) *adj.* connected with, bound to

sommaire *m.* summary; *adj.* summary, concise

somme *f.* sum

son *m.* sound

son, sa, ses *possessive adj.* his, her, its (i.e., **son** means "his," "her" or "its," depending on context; the same is true for **sa** and **ses**)

sorte *f.* sort, kind; **en quelque sorte** as it were

sortir *v.* (conjugated with **être**) to go out, come out; to take out (*see* Lesson I, paragraph 7)

soucier: se soucier de to be concerned about

soucieux, soucieuse *adj.* anxious

soude *f.* soda, caustic soda

soufre *m.* sulfur

soumettre *v.* to subject

sourd, sourde *adj.* deaf; **faire le sourd** to pretend to be deaf

sourire *v.* to smile; *n. m.* smile

soutenir *v.* to sustain

souvenir *v.* **se souvenir de** to remember; **souvenir** *n. m.* memory

souvent *adv.* often

spatial, spatiale *adj.* spatial

stylo *m.* fountain pen

subir *v.* to undergo, experience

suffire *v.* to be sufficient

suite *f.* consequence; follow-up; **à la suite de** following; **par la suite, à la suite** later, subsequently; **par suite de** in consequence of, as a result of

suivre *v.* to follow

sujet *m.* subject; **à ce sujet** about this matter, about this subject; **au sujet de** about, concerning

support *m.* support, base

sur *prep.* on, upon; **droit sur** straight at, straight toward; (*see* Appendix C for use of **sur** with numerals and dimensions)

surprendre *v.* to surprise

surtout *adv.* especially, chiefly

surveiller *v.* to keep an eye on, supervise

survenir *v.* to happen

susceptible *adj.* capable; likely to

syndicat *m.* labor union

synthèse *f.* synthesis

tableau *m.* picture, painting

tâche *f.* task

taire: se taire *v.* to be quiet, become quiet, quiet down, become silent

tant *adv.* so much, so many; **tant de gens** so many people

tante *f.* aunt

tapis *m.* rug

tard *adv.* late

technique *f.* technique; techniques, technology; *adj.* technical (*see* Lesson VIII, paragraph 4d)

tel, telle *adj.* such

temps *m.* time

tendrement *adv.* tenderly

tenir *v.* to hold; **tenir à** to be fond of, set great store by; to insist upon, to be anxious to; to be due to; **s'en tenir à** to stick to, limit oneself to, abide by; **tenir compte de** to take into account, bear in mind; **se tenir au courant** to keep oneself informed; **tenir des propos** to make some remarks

tenter *v.* to attempt; to tempt

terme *m.* termination; **mener à terme** bring to a conclusion

terre *f.* land; earth

thèse *f.* thesis

tirer *v.* to draw

titre *m.* title

toit *m.* roof

tomber *v.* (conjugated with **être**) to fall

tort *m.* wrong; **avoir tort** to be wrong

toujours *adv.* always; still

tout (**toute, tous, toutes**) *adj.* all, whole, entire; any, every; **tout** *pron.* everything (that); **tout** *adv.* quite, just; **tout le monde** everyone; **tout de suite** immediately; **tout à l'heure** just a minute ago, in just a minute; **tout d'abord** at first; **tout à fait** quite, entirely (*see* Lesson X, paragraph 4)

toutefois *adv.* however

traduire *v.* to translate

traiter *v.* to treat

tranquillité *f.* peace, tranquillity

transcrire *v.* to transcribe

transmettre *v.* to transmit, convey

travail (*pl.* **travaux**) *m.* work

travailler *v.* to work

traverse *f.* (railroad) tie

traverser *v.* to cross

très *adv.* very

triage *m.* siding, marshaling yard

triste *adj.* sad

tromper *v.* to deceive; **se tromper** to make a mistake

tronc *m.* tree trunk

trouver *v.* to find; **se trouver** to be located, to find oneself, to be

unir *v.* to join, combine, unite

usager *m.* user, consumer

utile *adj.* useful

utiliser *v.* to utilize, use

vaillant, vaillante *adj.* valiant

vaincre *v.* to overcome, vanquish

valable *adj.* valid, good

valeur *f.* value; **mettre en valeur** to develop, exploit, put into production, emphasize (a word)

valise *f.* valise, suitcase

valoir *v.* to be worth, to win, gain (especially in certain past tenses: *see* Lesson II, paragraph 5)

veille *f.* eve, the day (evening) before

vendre *v.* to sell

venir *v.* (conjugated with **être**) to come; **venir de** (+*inf.*) to have just (*see* Lesson IV, Idioms)

vent *m.* wind

venter *v.* (*impers.*) to be windy

vérité *f.* truth

vertigineux, vertigineuse *adj.* dizzying

vertu *f.* virtue

vide *adj.* empty; *m.* vacuum; empty space

vie *f.* life; living, livelihood

vieux (vieil, vieille, vieux, vieilles) *adj.* old

ville *f.* city, town; **en ville** in town, into town, to town

vingt twenty

visser *v.* to screw (down, on)

vite *adv.* quickly, fast

vitesse *f.* speed

vivre *v.* to live

voie *f.* road; track

voilà *adv.* there is, there are (for use with expressions of time, *see* Lesson III, paragraph 1)

voir *v.* to see

voisin *m.* neighbor

voiture *f.* car; coach

vol *m.* flight

voleur *m.* thief

vouloir *v.* to want, wish; (in some past tenses) to try to, start to, insist on, refuse to (with negative); would like (in conditional: **voudrais**), would have liked (in conditional perfect); **vouloir bien** to be willing, to consent; **vouloir dire** to mean; **en vouloir à** to be angry at, to bear a grudge against (*see* Lesson II)

voyage *m.* trip

voyageur *m.* traveler, passenger

vrai, vraie *adj.* true

vraisemblable *adj.* likely, probable

y *adv.* there; to it, to them; in it, in them, etc. (*see* Lesson IX)

yeux: *see* œil

INDEX

à, in relation to *y* and *lui*, 66–67

adjectives, plural, 52–53; irregular feminine, 53–54; with second masculine form, 54; used as nouns, 54; meaning according to position, 56–57; agreement, 57; comparative and superlative, 68; demonstrative, 71; requiring *de* before an infinitive, 105

adverbs, forms and uses, 74–75; adverbs listed, 110–12

agreement, of past participles, 6, 27; of adjectives, 57

article with adjective, 54

comparison of adjectives, 58–59

conditional and conditional perfect tenses, meaning, 4, 8 (footnote); of *devoir*, 32–34; special idiomatic uses, 87–88; in conditional sentences, 88–90

days of the week, 117–18

de, relation to *en*, 65–67; in idioms with verbs, 68–69; summary of uses, 103–05

demonstrative adjectives, 71

demonstrative pronouns, 71–73

depuis, with present and imperfect tenses, 17–18

devoir, uses and meanings, 32–34

dimensions, 117

dont, uses and meanings, 81–82

en, with *il faut*, 36; as a pronoun, 64–68; as a preposition, 18, 67; as merely an element of an idiom, 68

être, as auxiliary with certain intransitive verbs, 5–6; as auxiliary with reflexives, 26–27; rule for translation, 28–29

faire, causative, 46–48

falloir (*il faut*), uses and meanings, 34–36

false cognates, 113–14

future tense, distinguished from past, 3–4; future and future perfect showing probability, 87

grammatical terms defined, 119–22

historical present, 6

imperative of reflexive verbs, 27–28

imperfect indicative, contrasted with conditional, 4; meanings, 8–10; contrasted with other past tenses, 10–11; common errors in translating, 12–13; with *depuis*, *il y avait ... que*, 17–18

imperfect and pluperfect subjunctive, uses in conditional sentences 89–90; forms, 94; meanings, 89,95

impersonal verbs, 84

indefinite pronouns, *on*, 19; with subjunctive to express "whoever" and "whatever," 97; requiring *de* before an adjective, 105

infinitive, after a preposition, 18; reflexive, 27; negative, 42; preceded by *de* or *à*, 105

interrogative forms, meaning in present tense, 2; meaning in past indefinite, 3; reflexive verbs, 27–28

interrogative pronouns, 83–84

inversion, for interrogation, 2–3; in relative clauses, 80–81; after the conjunction *que*, 102; in conditional sentences, 90

measurement idioms, 117
mettre, idioms with, 20–21
months of the year, 118

negatives, 38–43
ne, 38–43; alone as negative, 42, 103; pleonastic, 42; in special idioms with *que*, 102, 103
nouns, irregular plurals, 52–53; noun-adjective word order, 55–57
numerals, 115–17

on, 19
orthographic changes in verbs, 130–31

partitive construction, 103–04
passive voice, 6, 28–29; expressed by active infinitive after *faire*, 46–49
past definite, distinguished from other tenses, 3–5
past indefinite, meanings, 3; of reflexives, 26–27, 29; of *pouvoir*, *vouloir*, *savoir*, etc., 11–12; of *devoir*, 32–33
past participle, with meaning of present participle or clause, 18–19; agreement, 6, 27
peu, 74–75
plural, nouns and adjectives, 52–53
pouvoir, meaning of past tenses, 12
prepositions, followed by infinitive, 18; *en*, 18, 67; *de*, 103–05; list of prepositions, 109–10
present indicative, meaning, 1–2; distinguished from past, 4–5; meaning "can," 6; historical present, 6; with *depuis*, *il y a . . . que*, 17

present participle, 18
present subjunctive, forms, 93–95; meanings, 95–98
probability, expressed by *devoir*, 33; expressed by future and future perfect, 87
pronouns, personal, 63–64; adverbial (*y*, *en*), 64–67; demonstrative, 71–73; relative, 80–83; interrogative, 83–84; indefinite, 19–20, 97

quand, *quand même* in idiomatic uses, 89, 90
quantity, words of, 104
que, uses summarized, 101–03

reciprocal pronouns, 26
reflexive pronouns, 26
reflexive verbs, 24–26
relative pronouns, 80–83

savoir, meanings of past tenses, 14
si in uses other than conditional sentences, 89, 90
subjunctive, forms 93–95; meanings in subordinate clauses, 95–98; in main clauses, 98; in conditional sentences, 98, 90

time of day, 117
tout, 75–76

verbs, conjugation of, Appendix E; impersonal use, 84

words often confused, 105–06

y, meanings, 66–67; as an element of an idiom, 68